WHAT DO I DO NOW?

Challenges and Choices for Camp Counselors and Other Youth Leaders

Jerome Beker
Doug Magnuson
Connie Magunson
David E. Beker

American Camping Association®

American Camping Association®
5000 State Road 67 North
Martinsville, IN 46151-7902
317/342-8456 American Camping Association Office
800/428-2267 American Camping Association Bookstore
317/342-2065 Fax

Library of Congress Cataloging-in-Publication Data
Beker, Jerome, 1933-
    What do I do now? : challenges and choices for camp counselors
and other youth leaders / Jerome Beker ... [et al.].
        p. cm.
    Updated version of: Training camp counselors in human relations.
    Includes index.
    ISBN 0-87603-151-3
    1. Camp counselors — United States. 2. Camp counselors —
Training of — United States. 3. Interpersonal relations — United
States. 4. Camping — United States — Case studies. I. Beker.
Jerome. II. American Camping Association. III. Training
counselors in human relations.
GV198.C6W48   1996
796.54 — dc20
                                            95-53712
                                            CIP

*To all our parents,
with love and appreciation
for introducing us to camping
and for so much more.*

Table of Contents

Part One:
The Use of Cases in Camping

Part Two: The Cases

Working within Program Activities and Routines

Working Professionally

Appendix

Preface

We have designed this book to make case study resources in the field of camping and suggestions for their use available to prospective camp staff members and to the people responsible for selecting, training, and supervising them. In addition, the material should be useful in a variety of other group-living, educational, and recreational settings. Readers familiar with the previous edition[1] may recognize some of the scenarios, but we have rewritten all of the retained cases and the material about the case study method and have added many new cases. We have updated both the language and the content to reflect changing realities on the threshold of a new century.

When May Cases Be Useful — and with Whom?

One way the cases may be used is to prepare prospective camp leaders who have had no previous camp experience as well as those who have been at camp but never in leadership positions. These people are entering a new situation or role, very different from their accustomed lives. Supervised analysis of cases can help to provide them with feelings of familiarity and security in making the necessary adjustments and in learning what kinds of behavior will be most effective.

The study of cases also provides an opportunity for more expe-

---

[1] Beker, Jerome. (1962). *Training Camp Counselors in Human Relations: A Case Book*. New York: Association Press.

rienced camp leaders to stand back and look with increased objectivity at their feelings and behavior at camp, especially when emotionally loaded problems and crises arise. Because of the closeness of interpersonal contact, as explained in chapter 1, seemingly slight misunderstandings can easily develop into major conflicts. Strong feelings are aroused when this happens, and it may be difficult for the people involved to regain their objectivity and perspective. At such times, a relevant case introduced for analysis can offer an external, somewhat less threatening stimulus for more objective, less emotional discussion.

We also anticipate that the book will be useful in college courses in camp counseling. It may serve as an adjunct textbook in general undergraduate or graduate camp counseling courses, as well as a primary resource in courses more specifically directed toward the leadership climate and the leadership process.

Further, there are many organizations whose year-round personnel are expected to serve in a camp setting during some part of the year. This is especially true in schools conducting school camping programs, where teachers with no camp experience may be expected to provide leadership. Many scouting and other organizations use part-time or volunteer leaders, including students, in the year-round program and employ some of the same people during the summer camping season even though they may lack camp leadership experience. In situations like these, organizations may find the cases useful in helping to prepare their personnel for camp responsibilities.

Although the emphasis in the use of the case study method has traditionally been (and is in this book) on pre- and in-service training and problem solving, readers may wish to explore other potential uses for the cases as well. For example, cases may be used in staff selection (with candidates asked to analyze a particular case or cases), in the evaluation of staff members or students, and to stimulate discussion and understanding among parents, campers, and others interested in the camping field. The detailed development of these "new frontiers" and additional applications of the material depend on the ingenuity and creativity of individual readers.

How to Use the Book

The book is organized to provide quick, easy access to material desired by readers with a variety of particular needs. Part 1 provides a detailed discussion of how to use the case study method in leadership training and problem solving, with an illustrative case analysis. The seven steps enumerated, to which frequent reference may be helpful, present the major elements in case analysis in outline form. An explanation of the appropriate use of the specific questions relating to each case, which appear in the Appendix, is included. Part 2 comprises the sixty cases included in the book.

A brief indication of the nature of each case is provided in the table of contents, where the cases are grouped according to their primary area of focus. In addition, there is a subject index of cases at the end of the book. Thus, selections among the cases, which range from relatively short and simple to quite complex, can easily be made to meet particular needs. Although the cases are largely based on actual occurrences or combinations of occurrences, all names of participants have, of course, been changed. Any resemblance between the names that appear in the cases and those of real people is, therefore, strictly coincidental.

Some of the language used by experienced camp people — camp jargon — may have little or no meaning, or even a different meaning, to people without organized camping experience. Even within the camping field, there are significant variations in terminology. For consistency, the term "cabin group" is used throughout the book to refer to the basic camp living group. Supervisors of counselors and direct care staff in various camps may be known as unit directors, division heads, group leaders, head counselors, program directors, and the like. We have used several of these, but readers can substitute their preferred designations.

As they become familiar with the nature and uses of open-end cases, camp leaders may wish to prepare additional cases based on their own experiences and situations specific to the setting involved. Developing such materials can also serve as a valuable training exercise, since the preparation of effective cases requires conscious effort to perceive and present complex interactions clearly and objectively.

The case study method requires more of the instructor or supervisor than do more traditional teaching techniques. He or she must be a sensitive leader with the patience and internal security to permit learners a large measure of freedom. The reward is the genuine satisfaction that derives from the experience of providing effective leadership and from the knowledge that one has played a vital role in the development of effective leaders.

A Note to the Counselor

Our purpose will be achieved if this book serves as a springboard for your personal growth as an effective leader and human relations practitioner. Beginning here, you will grow through your discussions and experiences at camp. The cases provide resources for "practice" while the stakes and emotional involvement are low. We hope that you will be able to identify with the people in the cases and that, when you are involved in actual situations, you will be able to maintain a comparable degree of objectivity. If the cases and your discussions of them help you gain this ability to stand off and observe a situation in which you are involved, they will have served well.

However, a large measure of this insight can be developed only through experience; cases and discussion may be able to make experience clearer and easier to interpret and evaluate, but they cannot replace it. Only by actually living a situation can we achieve the deepest understanding and "feel" of it. Nevertheless, although each situation is unique, cases can familiarize us with the application of underlying principles and prepare us to handle new situations more effectively.

We hope that you will find the cases and the discussions arising from them stimulating and helpful. They represent experiences that we all have in common: human interactions and emotions. The process will be useful in a practical sense, however, only to the extent to which you can apply it in your day-to-day work.

As you grow in competence in your relationships with campers, colleagues, and supervisors alike, you may be confident that you are attaining a new ability that will serve you well after camp and throughout your life. Situations are different, but there are significant commonalities among people of all ages and in all places. The skills that help you to be an effective counselor will also enhance your happiness and effectiveness in every other human relationship — in your family, your lifetime occupation, your neighborhood, your leisure-time groups, and in carrying out your obligations throughout life as a citizen and citizen-leader. Effective citizenship is, in fact, another way of looking at the whole subject.

In Conclusion

Organized camping has consistently attempted to adapt and apply useful techniques from other settings. It seems apparent that camping cases can provide their readers with vicarious experience in realistic situations of the kind they will be expected to deal with on the job, much as do cases in other fields. Thus, camp counselors, supervisors, and directors can be equipped to enhance the overall camp environment, to prevent and respond effectively to situations in which someone's personal or interpersonal environment has broken down, and to utilize any eventuality in the service of camper growth and development. We sincerely hope that this book will prove to be as valuable to the organized camping movement and to all of us young and not-so-young people who are involved in it together as such materials have in other fields.

— *JB, DM, CM, DEB*

In Appreciation

In the earlier edition of this book, which appeared over thirty years ago, acknowledgment was made of the substantive and technical contributions of a number of people who, thereby, contributed indirectly to this one as well, even though their names are not repeated here. We hereby acknowledge their roles collectively. Happily, most are still alive and active contributors, although the passing of mentors Sam Cooper and Ray Patouillet in particular is noted here with continuing sadness. Newcomers to the fold include several current camp directors — Mark Hennessy of Camp Pepin, Jeff Wubbles of Birchwood, Georgann Rumsey of Friendship Ventures, Brad Kunkler of Camp St. Croix, Leslie McCoy of Circle "R" Ranch, and Cheryl Hammers of Sanderson — whose suggestions for and about cases have not only added to the scope of the content, but also helped to validate its appropriateness and currency. We also appreciate the support, advice, and assistance of Grechen Throop, ACA's publications director, throughout the process and the careful manuscript proofreading by Ruth Beker. Finally, particular gratitude goes to Emily Beker, whose substantive, editorial, and technical contributions have enhanced and enriched what follows in many ways.

— JB, DM, CM, DEB

Part One

The Use
of Cases
in Camping

Chapter One

The Case Study Method

In both the selection and the training of leaders in any field, the primary concern is with their potential *behavior* in a leadership role rather than simply with what they know about leadership. Methods of selection and training involving actual participation in leadership situations are, therefore, usually most effective, but they are frequently impracticable. It is in this context that the case study approach has proved to be most useful, since it is but one step removed from actual participation. Thus, case study and analysis permit us to respond to some extent as if we were really involved in the situation portrayed, rather than responding only in terms of abstract ideas and principles.

This approach, a proven tool for the enhancement of relationships and effectiveness in groups, has been adapted to such fields as education, social work, psychological counseling, law, business, industry, and the armed forces. Its appropriateness for increasing the effectiveness of youth leaders and others who work with people in activity-based, developmentally oriented settings such as organized camping seems clear intuitively and has become evident in practice with the earlier edition of this book and other such resources. *Fifty Cases for Camp Counselors*[1] antedated the development of the case study method on which current practice is based, but it provides a good example of the sustained appeal of this approach over at least half a century.

---

[1]Ure, R. W. (1946). New York: Association Press.

What Is a Case?

The cases are narratives of significant situations that have occurred, or could have occurred, at camp. Many were handled unsuccessfully when they arose. Only the immediate circumstances are given, together with such background information as may be necessary for clarification. We have intentionally omitted what was actually done, or could have been done, and the outcomes. Thus the cases are "open-ended," presenting a situational and emotional context and stopping at a point where a decision must be made by at least one of the people portrayed. The reader is presented with an emergency requiring immediate action or an opportunity to provide a constructive experience for campers, for colleagues, and/or for him or herself. Such crisis situations frequently contain the seeds of human growth; whether they turn out to be stepping stones or stumbling blocks depends on how they are handled by the people involved.

The cases typically present problems to be solved, which need to be viewed from the perspectives of all the significant actors and on at least two levels: the immediate problem and the broader or longer-term issues. The latter include consequences for the growth and development of all concerned and for the enhancement of the life of the group. Those using the cases are expected to analyze them and to make the necessary decisions in the context of complex human relationships, program objectives, and their own fundamental principles, beliefs, and values.

As is usually true in actual situations that arise at camp, the cases have no single "right" answers. Problems must be handled in accordance with the personalities and needs of the people involved, always in the light of camp objectives and basic values. In practice, although many crises must be addressed immediately, more comprehensive solutions must frequently be developed over a period of time. Anticipating such situations and intervening so that they do not arise in the first place is usually the best "solution" of all, and it is useful to consider how the crisis could have been prevented as well as how it might best be handled.

Of course, most of the cases do not portray the smoothness and warmth that pervade so much of camp life; rather, their function is to illuminate some of the kinds of difficulties that arise from time to time, places where counselors often get "stuck." Those of you with camp experience will probably recognize some of the situations as similar to ones in which you have been involved.

Why Case Studies in Camping?

The importance of the quality and content of human interactions and leadership in the successful functioning of any organization or enterprise that requires the coordinated efforts of people is abundantly clear in all kinds of group work situations. This is especially evident in organized camping, since people at camp live together very closely in a setting designed to have a positive developmental impact on those involved.

We can escape from an uncomfortable situation at school or at the office when we go home for the evening and on weekends. At home, our deep emotional ties help us to accept each other even in the face of marked conflicts, but we do in fact spend most of our waking hours away from the family. As a camp staff member, however, each of us lives, works, plays, eats, and sleeps with the same people — many of them unfamiliar to us at first — day after day, with relatively little interruption. Only other types of residential institutions (including the armed services) are comparable in this respect. The relatively primitive camp environment also throws us into much closer physical and emotional proximity than that to which we are usually accustomed. Therefore, the potential for the development of interpersonal conflict and even hostility is evident.

There is little or no chance for such friction, once developed, to dissipate, since the people involved are in such close and constant contact. On the contrary, a negative relationship can easily get "into a rut," feeding on itself and becoming more and more unpleasant and harmful to the organization and to the people involved. Nor do we want to encourage people to build emotional walls around themselves to shut out the reality of interpersonal relations in a camp environment, so every effort must be made to sustain healthy human relations. Since cases have been found to be useful in training individuals and groups in good human relations and effective leadership, both of which are essential qualities in organized camping, their potential value in the camp context seems clear.

Compounding the situation is the fact that, unlike many other group living situations, the impact of the experience on the development of those involved constitutes the primary purpose — the raison d'etre — of the entire enterprise. Whether the program is designed to serve a special population that exhibits particular developmental difficulties or "normal" youth, it seeks through a primarily "fun" experience to facilitate and enhance the physical, mental, emotional, social, spiritual, and moral growth of its clientele. Thus, the focus is on effective human relations in the service of these larger objectives. Cases offer the opportunity to consider the growth-enhancing and growth-retarding potential of alternative intervention options without putting people at risk in a real situation.

In addition, the use of cases to explore and clarify difficult real situations as they arise can help to divert attention from the actual conflict situation and the people involved, so that feelings that may be blocking solutions have a chance to begin to subside. Meanwhile, the participants may be able to see parallels between the case being analyzed and the actual situation in which they are involved. This process frequently enables them to attain greater objectivity and perspective. Tensions are decreased as a result, and solutions acceptable to all concerned are more easily reached, thus tending to dissipate threats to camp functioning. Sensitive supervisors may sometimes decide that permitting a particular situation to run its course, even through a violent altercation, is a better approach, but cases provide an additional alternative for them to use if they wish.

The Case Study Process

Careful study of the cases will reveal that there are surprisingly many ways of looking at each. The various characters in a given case may perceive the situation differently. From his or her own frame of reference, the view held by each is understandable. As this becomes clear, you can begin to establish the habit of seeking the solution to a crisis rather than merely seeking someone on whom to place the blame. This is much more difficult to do when one is actually involved in a situation, and case study helps learners (using "safe," somewhat impersonal materials) to develop the ability to stand back and observe situations objectively before making decisions.

The cases provide a somewhat limited picture; just as in actual situations, we do not know all the facts and must identify problems, make decisions, and take action based on partial knowledge. Thus, skills in analysis and inference are stimulated. We can give operational meaning to abstract, verbal principles of leadership.

We suggest that, for the best results, the cases should be read and analyzed by individuals separately and then further analyzed and discussed in groups of between five and ten people, as we describe in more detail following the listing of recommended steps in case analysis provided below. When individuals have read a case in advance, thought about it, and decided how they would handle it, subsequent group discussion is usually of greater value.

Steps in Case Analysis

There are seven steps in case analysis. It may be helpful to discuss your analysis and conclusions with others, such as colleagues or supervisors. You may also wish to use the table of contents and the index to identify other cases that raise similar issues, perhaps in more complex form, or to draw on your own experiences, for comparative purposes. Reconsideration of the same case after a time lapse may lead to additional insights as well.

Group Analysis of Cases

Group analysis of cases can help individuals broaden and deepen their understanding in several ways. First, the underlying motivations of various characters and the consequences of their possible courses of action usually become clearer as some group members contribute insights that others had overlooked. As members identify, consciously or unconsciously, with the characters described, other group members may become better able to visualize the situations portrayed from a variety of perspectives. Methods such as role playing can be used to facilitate this process.

Seven Steps in Case Analysis

1. Read and think about the case, seeking to identify the immediate problem or crisis and the deeper issues that seem to be involved.

2. Try to understand the needs and feelings of each of the characters portrayed or implied in the case and why they do what they do.

3. Identify any characters whom you may favor, dislike, praise, or blame. Try to understand your reaction, and try to avoid being biased for or against them.

4. Determine the present alternatives and the probable short- and long-range outcomes of each.

5. Given the situation as presented, decide what specific action, if any, should be taken, and why.

6. Consider the questions provided in the Appendix to see if they suggest any issues or insights that you may have overlooked. Questions for each case are provided in the Appendix.

7. Consider how the problem or problems might have been foreseen and prevented.

Case analysis places the responsibility for learning where it belongs — on the learner. This is especially true in group analysis, where each individual is expected to contribute to the success of a group effort for the benefit of all, just as at camp itself. Learners can begin to see themselves as collaborators with their instructors and supervisors, working toward common goals, rather than as "sponges" absorbing knowledge flowing from above, which would not promote effective leadership.

In addition, effective camp leadership requires a feeling of camaraderie and joint responsibility for the realization of objectives shared by leaders and campers. Only as prospective leaders learn to function in this kind of relationship to authority figures will they be able to work comfortably and effectively with their campers. Group analysis of cases with an instructor frequently and sometimes dramatically helps learners overcome irrational fears of authority. Thus, the very mutuality between teachers and learners that is fostered by group study of cases plays an important role in the leadership development process.

It is not only with regard to authority that group analysis of cases provides prospective leaders with opportunities to improve their patterns of relationship and thereby their leadership potential, but also with regard to other elements of interpersonal interaction. On one level, group discussion of a case is centered on the content of the case itself. At the same time, however, the participants in the discussion are involved in a group situation and, consciously or unconsciously, are taking various roles that promote or impede the group's progress toward its goals. It is easy to see how closely this situation resembles that at camp, where the effectiveness of the enterprise also depends on the behavior of the people involved in it. The case provides a focus for the group effort, but it is important to pay attention to what is happening in the group as well as to the case if the full learning potential of group case analysis is to be realized.

Chapter Two

An Illustrative Case

The following short, seemingly simple case and the accompanying discussion are provided as an example, to help make the methods of case analysis more concrete and meaningful. The numbers that appear in parentheses refer readers to the appropriate steps in the process as they are listed in chapter 1. It should also be noted that the material that follows sometimes extrapolates liberally from what is directly presented in the case to highlight and clarify the kinds of underlying factors that may (or may not) be at work.

A Rookie's Predicament

Jim and his campers were meandering toward the craft shop, at the opposite end of camp, where Jim was assigned to assist with his group that morning.

He was thinking about camp as he walked. The season, his first as a counselor, had opened a week ago. He enjoyed the responsibility and challenge and was anxious to do well, to "prove himself." In fact, his enthusiasm had caused him to get completely absorbed in what he was doing — so absorbed that he had forgotten himself several times and been late for his next assignment as a result. Jim felt that this was only partly his fault, but Hank, his supervisor, had asked him more than once to make a special effort to be more prompt.

These thoughts were suddenly interrupted as Davey, an eleven-year-old in his cabin group, called him aside, obviously trying to hide the fact that he was crying. He asked Jim if they could find a place to talk alone. Jim recalled that Davey was the only new camper in his group and was away from home for the first time. The only staff member in sight was Beth, an off-duty counselor, who was walking up the steps of the counselors' retreat.

Analyzing "A Rookie's Predicament"

_____ *STEP 1* _____

The first step is, of course, to *read the case*. This should be followed by a more detailed study of the material, which can be approached from many points of view.

To begin, it may be helpful to decide and list what the problem or problems seem to be. It is also important, however, to remain alert to new possibilities that frequently present themselves during the process. In "A Rookie's Predicament," for example, the following problem areas may be identified, at least as possibilities:

- Jim's adjustment in his new job
- Davey's adjustment to camp
- The attitude of experienced campers in Davey's cabin group

Can you think of any others?

_____ *STEP 2* _____

In analyzing a case, one should *attempt to infer the perspectives of each of the characters portrayed, so as to illuminate why they did what they did.* Thus, the habit of seeking to understand the reasons for behavior — a necessary prerequisite for successful functioning in any leadership role — can be developed. Some possible reasons for the behavior of the various characters in "A Rookie's Predicament" are suggested below:

> Jim *was anxious to do well, to "prove himself."* Suddenly he finds himself faced with a situation in which his natural inclination as a sensitive counselor, to stay with Davey, is in conflict with what his supervisor seems to expect from him. To deal with the situation effectively, Jim must try to understand the perspectives of the people involved. Lacking more detailed knowledge about them, he is forced to hypothesize on the basis of what he does know, being ever alert to the significance of new information.

Davey was the only new camper in his group and was away from home for the first time. Homesickness would be a possibility. Perhaps the other boys had been making things difficult for him, the only stranger among them. Maybe he was having one of those days when everything seems to go wrong, and he may have been the only camper in the cabin not to have gotten mail from either of his parents, who were in the process of getting a divorce. Or perhaps he had! This and homesickness could have combined to overwhelm him. Jim may be the only person in camp with whom he has established a relationship and the only one in whom he feels he can confide. What other likely possibilities are there?

Jim felt that this was only partly his fault, but his supervisor had asked him several times to make a special effort to be more prompt. Hank, the supervisor, probably felt that some of the counselors in his unit were becoming too lax about their responsibilities. Perhaps the director had noticed this and criticized Hank for it. Hank had emphasized the importance of promptness in several chats with Jim, the worst offender. He knew that Jim was late only because he was busy on other camp work, but he felt that it was very important that Jim learn better timing so as not to delay activities unnecessarily or to put campers at risk.

The only staff member in sight was Beth, an off-duty counselor, who was walking up the steps... Perhaps she was very tired, badly in need of some time away from the campers, or had an urgent letter to write. Free for maybe the first time in days, she could have been deep in personal thoughts as she approached the counselor's retreat.

Jim and his campers were meandering toward the craft shop.... The campers knew that the crafts specialist would not allow them to start until Jim arrived, because they had been delayed on several other occasions when he was late. They would be able to see that it was Davey who was delaying Jim this time. Quite possibly, they resented Davey's "intrusion" into their group this season. He was a new camper and unskilled in many of the things that were important to them.

In addition, it is often necessary to consider the feelings of characters not directly portrayed in the case, but whose existence and influence can logically be inferred. As you think about and discuss such hypothetical possibilities as the following, the overall dynamics of a situation may come into sharper focus, enabling it to be handled more effectively.

The crafts specialist may have learned that assistance was required to get groups started effectively. In addition, he has probably found that counselors sometimes did not arrive at all unless he made sure that they were there. Quite possibly, the camp director has asked him to insist that the counselor assigned to each group be present before the program could be started for that group.

The camp director may be rather pleased with the season so far, except for one unit that has been too slow in getting to activities and has seemed generally to be wasting too much time to get the maximum benefit from the camp experience. She may have already spoken to the unit supervisor about this. Now she sees a group of campers walking slowly toward the crafts shop and their counselor far behind them, talking with a single camper who has no particular problems that the director is aware of.

Davey's parents may recognize that it is difficult for him to adjust to his first experience away from home. Perhaps they have received letters indicating that he is trying to overcome his feelings of homesickness with the help of one counselor to whom he feels especially close — Jim. Although they are preoccupied with their own problems, the parents are also worried about Davey and grateful to Jim for what he has been able to do. They feel that they can depend on him to help Davey get through this difficult period, and they have told him so.

_____ STEP 3 _____

It is important that the reader seek to identify and understand his or her feelings about the main character — the one on whom the case is focused — and the others whose roles are portrayed. This is part of the process of developing objectivity, and it requires conscious effort. Efforts of this kind can help staff learn to become aware of the pulls affecting each individual involved in a situation — knowledge that can contribute to making a more effective leader and colleague.

Some people will find themselves selecting a scapegoat, a character on whom to place the blame for whatever problem situation has developed. At this point, the reader might wonder why his or her thinking has developed in this direction and what good can come from fixing the blame. Does this lead to a solution of the problem? Might there be a more positive and constructive approach?

> Jim may feel that Hank is taking too narrow a view of a counselor's role or is simply being unfair. But if Jim stops to think that Hank (a) is really trying to help him develop better timing and (b) may be under pressure from the director, he may be less inclined to blame Hank for the situation. It is clear that for Jim to react with resentment toward Hank would not help Davey, nor would it help Jim's relationships at camp.

Note that the same kind of thinking can be applied to each character from the point of view of any of the others. The point being made is not that feelings of blame and resentment should be suppressed, but that they frequently can be avoided if an honest effort is made to understand the perspectives of each participant in a given situation. This is not a solution to "A Rookie's Predicament," but it clears the way for rational thought and appropriate decision making.

The case also provides an illustration of the importance of considering most situations on two levels. The immediate crisis may be obvious. In addition, however, there is the ongoing issue of the behavior and the relationships involved in the context of the larger goals of the program.

Jim is presented with a situation in which he must decide quickly how best to help Davey and at the same time meet his other responsibilities, if possible. More fundamentally, Jim must work out his relationships with each of the people involved and with his job responsibilities, with an eye toward the long-range developmental objectives of the camp experience for each of the campers.

_____ *STEP 4* _____

It is also important to *determine what courses of action are available to the focal character — usually a counselor — at the point where a case description ends, and what would be the likely outcomes of each.* For example, what would have been the probable results (for all of those involved) if Jim had:

...asked Davey to wait and speak with him later about whatever was bothering him?

...taken a walk with Davey to talk, as Davey had asked him to do?

...asked Davey to talk while they walked to the crafts shop, where the rest of the cabin group would be waiting?

...asked Davey to talk with the counselor walking into the counselors' retreat?

...called the counselor going into the counselors' retreat and asked her to substitute for him at crafts for a while?

...asked Davey to wait there or in the cabin until Jim could arrange to leave his crafts assignment?

...tried to locate the supervisor or director to explain the situation?

...called to the stragglers he saw still walking toward the craft shop to tell them that he would be late and asked them to try to get started without him?

What other alternatives are open to Jim?

_____ *STEP 5* _____

The reader should then make a clear decision regarding what he or she would actually do *in the situation portrayed in the case and why*. This makes the exercise more realistic and gives it focus since, in an actual situation, a decision must be made. To vacillate and make no decision is, in effect, a decision in itself and, in most crises, a poor one.

It should be noted that there is frequently no ideal decision, no complete solution to the problem. Effective leaders must be able to act in the face of uncertainty and often with the understanding that they are selecting only the least dangerous or distasteful of a series of poor alternatives.

The case analysis method outlined earlier is largely an organized procedure for arriving at the best decision possible given the circumstances, but in real situations there is rarely time for such detailed analyses before making at least tentative decisions. Therefore, it is important to develop the habit of analytic thinking so that it occurs almost automatically and sound decisions can be made in a crisis.

_____ *STEP 6* _____

Questions pertinent to each case appear in the Appendix and are provided as additional stimulants to thought and to help you focus attention on basic, underlying issues. They refer to significant aspects and implications of a particular case that might otherwise be overlooked, including ethical considerations implicit in the situations portrayed. They are intended only as suggestions, however, and are not meant to precede or constrict the process of analysis outlined here.

The questions can usually be most helpful at this point in the process rather than earlier, lest they stifle rather than expand thought. Here, they may suggest new perspectives and issues that had not previously been considered. The following questions might have been among those listed for "A Rookie's Predicament" had it been presented as one of the cases for analysis in this book:

- Fundamentally, is it Jim's responsibility to do what his supervisor has asked?

- To do what seems to be best for Davey?
- Which of these should take precedence? Why?

<hr>
_____ *STEP 7* _____

The question of *how the crisis portrayed in the case could have been prevented should be considered in detail as an integral part of case analysis*. In any such situation, it may be that one or more participants are not in harmony with the goals of the enterprise in which the group is engaged, or they may be incompetent, mentally ill, or both. Only infrequently, however, can such factors fairly be said to be the sole cause of the problem, thus rendering the preventive efforts of others largely futile. Even when such factors are present, the short-term situation is typically out of the counselor's control. He or she must function as well as possible to prevent further damage. In any event, it seems clear that finding someone to blame — a scapegoat — is usually not the most effective way to solve the immediate problem faced in a crisis. It is only when we consider long-range goals and prevention that the "blame" concept may occasionally prove helpful.

If the crafts counselor is really unable to control the group and is generally incompetent, for example, there is typically little that a young counselor like Jim can do about the situation, at least until some change is made, except to work with that person as best he can. Jim may (and should) discuss it with his supervisor if the crafts program for his group seems ineffective. But to blame all his difficulties on someone else would do nothing to solve the immediate problem and could cause staff dissension leading to more serious conflicts. The point here is that there is a difference between necessary and proper professional criticism and attempts to solve a problem in the context of present reality.

Consideration of how the crisis could have been foreseen and forestalled is essential, since such problems have a way of mushrooming. This is especially so at camp where, as we have seen above, interpersonal contacts are so close. When a crisis develops, even optimum handling may leave a residue of negative feeling that can erupt in greater difficulties later. Once begun, a cycle of this sort is difficult to stop, since greater problems require more drastic action, which tends to leave even more potential for conflict than was present before. At the same time, it should be recognized that resolving a serious problem situation constructively may (and should) be a positive learning experience that can lead to a continuing process of personal growth for all concerned.

Prevention may be considered on different levels, depending on how far back you go in time and the point of view from which you examine the situation. It may be most valuable to the prospective counselor to consider, at least at first, what he or she could have done to foresee and forestall the crisis.

> Perhaps the immediate crisis could have been prevented if Jim had been able to sense Davey's feelings earlier and helped him come to grips with his problems before he reached the breaking point. Such an effort might have included an approach through the other members of the group, since they may not be helping Davey to become involved with them. From another point of view, the immediate situation would have presented no crisis if Jim's reputation and relationships were such that his lateness at the crafts shop would be understood and accepted. How might Jim have accomplished this?

It is usually helpful to make notes, however rough, in developing a case analysis. Making comparisons with other cases, perhaps identified through the descriptions in the table of contents and the index and with your own experience may add new perspectives. Informal discussion of cases with colleagues and supervisors can also broaden and deepen understandings. If it is possible to return to a case and analyze it again after a lapse of time, interesting insights may result from a comparison of the two analyses. Perhaps surprisingly, there can be marked differences, and you can often see evidence of individual growth in this kind of exercise. Any discrepancies should, of course, be studied until they are understood.

Group Analysis of Techniques

When an individual has carefully analyzed a case in these ways, he or she should be well prepared to reap maximum benefit from participation in a group effort to analyze the same material, for the reasons described at the end of chapter 1.

The process of group case analysis includes the same general analytic procedures that have been outlined above and permits even greater breadth and depth of understanding and growth. A new dimension that must be considered by the group members, in addition to the case being discussed, is the development of human relations within the group itself. Thus the group method provides a "double-barreled" approach to human relations learning.

The procedure followed in group analysis of cases usually parallels that used in individual analysis, except that the insights of different individuals can be pooled, discussed, and reevaluated in the group.

We should note that, although group consensus in any or all of these areas may be desirable, it is by no means a required outcome of group case analysis. On the contrary, no individual should be pressured to join in a consensus of opinion so long as he believes himself to possess a significantly different and valid insight. On the other hand, individuals are responsible to the group not to permit personal, irrelevant, or emotional factors to obstruct its actions. It is here that the group approach serves on a different level, by providing the group members with an actual human relations situation in which they can practice and develop effective behavior. Thus, there is an analogy between cases for discussion and the discussion group itself.

In "A Rookie's Predicament," Jim could become resentful of his supervisor and insist on doing things his own way, thus disrupting the camp program to some extent. Or he could suppress the feeling that Davey needs his help and go along with his supervisor's stress on promptness. It is probable that neither of these reactions would be wise and in the best interests of Davey, the camp, the supervisor, or

Jim's feelings of well-being. Therefore, Jim might do best to respect his own insight into Davey's need for help, and at the same time to try to meet his responsibilities to the larger group.

Likewise, an effective discussion group member must have the ability to judge when the greatest good will be served by "going along" and when the importance of the issue involved exceeds that of harmony, so that one must maintain a minority position. In the camp situation, of course, considerations of professional ethics determine the avenues through which such disagreements may legitimately be expressed.

In this context, the case material serves as the focus around which the group experience is centered. It is important that the group be aware of its own functioning. The roles taken by each member at various times and their appropriateness or inappropriateness should be studied and discussed. The learning process can be greatly facilitated if a trained and experienced discussion leader can work with each group, but groups can function effectively even without this resource.

Whether a leader is provided or leadership emerges from within the group itself, or both, it is important that an atmosphere of freedom and spontaneity be maintained. Fear is a particularly strong barrier to learning in a group situation. Leadership properly includes encouraging broad participation, helping to maintain a degree of focus, stimulating deeper thought and interpretation, clarifying or summarizing when appropriate, and the like. The role of leadership, at least in this kind of situation, is to help the group achieve its goals. Leaders must inspire self-confidence and a willingness to contribute rather than fear and reticence. They are not present to impose their own interpretation of a situation on the group (nor should anyone else do this), and they should encourage the group to find its own answers rather than to depend upon the leader.[1]

---

[1] A detailed discussion of the leadership role is beyond the scope of this book, but we urge you to consult competent references on leadership.

It is also primarily up to the group to control and limit its members, but this should occur only in extreme cases, since apparent eccentricity may frequently have something to offer that the group will later find it needs. Of course, it is also important that most or all group members share the same motivation: to learn through the experience. Similarly, effective human relations cannot be established and maintained at camp unless most of the people involved are striving to achieve the same general goals and subscribe to nonconflicting values.

Given the necessary common goals, there are two general sources of interpersonal problems, both as portrayed in cases and as found in discussion groups. One relates to the emotional factors within one or more individuals, leading to various kinds of conflicts or withdrawals from the situation. More frequently, however, such difficulties develop from misunderstandings of the perspectives and roles of the various people involved. This is more closely related to emotional factors than it may appear to be, but the separation is helpful for purposes of analysis.

> If Jim fully understood Hank's situation, point of view, and the other pressures upon him, and if Hank were aware of Davey's approach to Jim at the moment described in "A Rookie's Predicament," might they have been more likely to have agreed on how Jim should respond?

Small groups of five to ten people are most effective in case analysis. A variety of viewpoints can be expressed, but at the same time there is ample opportunity for all in the group to participate. When larger numbers are involved, such as in college classes, it is best to divide the class into discussion groups of more convenient size. If there is more than one discussion group, it is often helpful to compare conclusions at the close of the discussion period.

There is value in establishing heterogeneous groups when circumstances permit. A group including, for example, two or three counselors, a specialist, a parent or two, a director, a former camper, and perhaps a camp nurse will tend to promote deeper and more effective learning than will a group composed completely of prospective cabin counselors. Frequently this will not be practicable, but even a group of prospective counselors is likely to include one or more former campers and one or more future specialists. The group leader or instructor may well be or have been a specialist, camp director, and/or a parent. Thus, a certain degree of heterogeneity is usually present even in a group seemingly rather homogeneous in outlook and prospective role at camp, such as a college class in camp counseling.

The technique of role playing provides an effective method of artificially reconstructing a variety of viewpoints and presenting them for consideration. The roles of characters portrayed in a case are assigned to various group members, who then act out the case while any remaining members observe. To promote maximum effectiveness, each actor should be given a few minutes beforehand to think about his or her role. After the role-playing experience, the situation may be discussed and the feelings of the various participants and observers compared. This method has proved to be effective in stimulating increased sensitivity and insight in human relations.

There are many variations and adaptations of role playing that may be used to facilitate learning. Some groups will wish to enact a given case more than once, with the roles rotated among different group members. It is frequently most helpful to keep all characters constant with the exception of one (the counselor or a camper, for example), on whom the group may wish to focus its subsequent discussion. Conversely, the group may wish to keep the enactor of a key role constant while other roles are rotated, in an attempt to observe how the same person's feelings and behavior may vary depending on how others act toward him. Role playing is, of course, a learning technique with much deeper and more complex potentialities than can be indicated here.

Additional techniques may be introduced as desired to enhance learning. For example, it is often helpful for group members to serve on a rotating basis as discussion leaders to gain leadership experience or as nonparticipant observers. Such observers can then report to the other members how they performed individually and as a group as seen from "outside." This may help to provide new insights for all concerned.

In short, the cases provide a focus for discussion and for the "cooperative competitiveness" of ideas that stimulates thinking and the progress of any group toward its goals. Group members learn to look at problems from the points of view of various other people. They learn to formulate and express their own opinions, when and how to defend them in the competition of ideas, and when and how to accept gracefully the ideas of others. Experience suggests that this process can lead to growth in the personal attitudes and insights of motivated participants, thus enhancing their effectiveness in leadership roles at camp and elsewhere.

Guide to the Selection of Cases

By their very nature, open-end cases are generally difficult to classify because they illustrate the interplay of the many issues that are typically involved in real-life situations. One-dimensional problems are usually unrealistic, because life rarely works that way. Thus, the cases that follow are multidimensional, but they are classified for your convenience according to the nature of the immediate decision or broader consideration called for at the end of the case. Within each case, however, we will note that additional issues are relevant and need to be considered as well if a successful resolution is to be attained.

There are three ways to select a case appropriate to a specific need. The case titles and brief descriptions that appear in the table of contents provide a quick screening tool. The five section titles, also in the table of contents, identify broader areas of focus (although most of the cases are relevant to more than one of those areas). They include working with individuals, groups, program issues, professional responsibilities, and parents. Finally, the index at the back of the book references the cases by topic. For example, if you are looking for a case about the use of alcohol, the index will refer you to "Out of Bounds."

No attempt is made to present every possible eventuality; that would be impossible. Instead, the cases have been selected because they provide an opportunity to illuminate the kinds of perspectives and strategies counselors need to be successful. For example, although there is no case specifically about the problem of campers who gamble, several cases relate to values, rules, discipline, and the like. Thus, the objective is not to train counselors in precisely what to do in a particular situation, but to educate them so that they will be able to use good judgment and appropriate techniques in responding to a wide variety of situations.

You may observe that almost all the cases focus on problematic or conflictual situations. This is because some level of conflict is needed to provoke interest and thought and because problematic situations often graphically illustrate key principles. It should not be assumed, however, that conflicts and problems entirely or even primarily define the counselor's role. In fact, if the cases are used effectively, the counselor should encounter fewer and less intense problems over time. As the last step of the proposed case analysis process suggests, discussion should provide insights into how problematic situations can be anticipated and avoided.

As another way to encourage staff members to generalize the lessons that can be drawn from case analysis, questions are provided in the Appendix for each case to help users to reflect more deeply on the issues involved and their implications.

Part Two

The Cases

The Cases

Working with Campers as Individuals

1. Virtual Kid

Sam exploded out of the car and into the cabin. His mother, Mrs. Martin, followed more slowly and introduced herself to Jordan. "And that flash you saw is Sam. He's really excited about being at camp. He's a pretty good kid and loves to have fun, but he's high energy. He has medication to help keep him under control."

Jordan helped Sam to get his things moved in. "We should check in with the nurse and drop off his medicine," he told Mrs. Martin. "She monitors special medical instructions. But other than that, he's all set."

After that had been done, Mrs. Martin prepared to leave. "Bye Sam, see you next week."

"Bye, Mom," Sam yelled from the other side of the cabin, where he was already involved in a game of marbles with two other boys and engaged in a loud conversation about baseball with yet another. "See you later!"

Mrs. Martin smiled a little ruefully as she walked away, and Jordan turned his attention to other new arrivals.

That evening, he lay in bed exhausted. The boys had not stopped running since they arrived, and their energy level seemed to be fueled by their excitement about being at camp and by Sam in particular. At dinner he had kept everyone within three tables entertained by holding up a barbecued chicken wing and clucking like a chicken in distress. Jordan chuckled at the memory. He knew he wasn't going to have trouble keeping them entertained. They were finding plenty of things to do, but he wasn't sure that he would be able to keep up with them.

Two days later, Jordan no longer felt like chuckling. Sam was indeed a source of energy who fired up the entire group. When things were going well, the boy's energy was contagious and the group rode that energy enthusiastically through the day's activities. But when things weren't going well, he fueled activities that destroyed morale and crippled the group's cohesiveness.

Jordan also sensed that Sam had the potential to push the group's judgment over the edge, perhaps creating a dangerous situation. The only corrective action that Sam seemed to understand was a combination of very tight behavioral limits and a high level of attention. But the demands on Jordan of maintaining that kind of environment were wearing him out. If I'm this tired now, what is it going to be like in three or four days? Jordan wondered. I'm not sure I can keep up.

Later that day he mentioned his problem to Leah, his supervisor. "What kind of help do you need?" she asked sympathetically.

"I think life would be easier if Sam weren't in the cabin. He's more than one person can handle, along with all the other boys. The rest of them would be easier to deal with without his influence. When he's good, he keeps everyone entertained, but when he's bad, he's really scary."

"Yes, I'm sure that's true," agreed Leah. "He's a real challenge, but I don't think we have a group where he wouldn't be even more disruptive at this point, and you're one of the best counselors we have. And he hasn't done anything that would justify sending him home. I can probably help out a little by hanging around with your group more than I have been. But let's see how things go now that we're a few days into camp. Maybe he'll calm down and the other boys will be less influenced by him."

Jordan was obviously skeptical. "I just feel that something bad is going to happen unless something is done."

"Something bad like what, Jordan?"

"I'm not sure. Maybe someone will get hurt, or something like that."

Leah didn't respond to that statement. "Let's see how it goes. I'll arrange to spend more time with you, and we'll try to get you some relief or additional time off when we can."

Why did I have to get this kid? Jordan thought as he walked back toward his cabin. I'm not sure how much more of his energy I can take. I just wish he had ended up in someone else's group or not come to camp at all. As he approached the cabin, he heard a scream of terror; as he entered, he saw one of his boys, Mookie, being held upside down by the ankles from the top bunk of a double-decker bed. Sam and Tommy were up there with him, each holding one of Mookie's ankles. The other boys were running around in a circle and slapping him in the face as they went by. Mookie was struggling to get free, but his struggles were only threatening to get him dropped to the floor on his head.

Jordan ran over and grabbed Mookie by the waist. "All right, that's enough," he shouted. "Knock it off!" He paused for a moment to collect his thoughts, turned Mookie right side up, and lowered him to the floor.

2. Sideline Sally

Sally was an introverted child, so much so that she appeared to have almost no social inclinations or interests. She did not appear to have problems in other respects, and on rare occasions she demonstrated a nice sense of humor. "Sally, do you want to play?" asked Nina, her counselor. "We need another player. It's fun!"

"No, I'd rather sit here. I'm not interested in the game."

Sally had not participated in any group activity, and at the beach she had waded around in the shallow area by herself. Her behavior was not offensive to anyone — the other girls already assumed that Sally was not going to be involved so they ignored her, and Nina sometimes thought wistfully that her job would be easier if the other girls were a little more introverted, too. But Nina felt that Sally was not gaining much from the camp experience and that Sally's non-participation was as much of a challenge to her counseling abilities as her active misbehavior would have been. She decided to try one more time. "But you haven't done anything since you got here, and it's the third day of camp!" Her exasperation showed in her voice. "Why did you come if you aren't going to do anything?" As soon as she heard herself say it, she regretted it.

Sally's response was firm and even more adamant. "I'm not hurting anybody and I'd rather not play, so please leave me alone."

Nina regrouped. "Sally, is there something wrong that you'd like to talk about? Is there anything we can do to help? Is there something I should know?" She was groping for ideas.

"No."

"Okay, I give up. Enjoy yourself." Nina turned her attention to the other girls, thinking that Sally was harder to figure out than even the worst misbehavior problem Nina had ever had. She did not know what to do, but she could not stop thinking about it, either.

3. Boo-Boo. Boo Hoo?

Dominick finished the ghost story by pausing for a long time to let it sink in, then he whispered a quick good night. The lights in the cabin were already off so that the story would seem scarier. The cabin was quiet and Dominick drifted off to sleep, satisfied that the boys were safely through another day.

After what seemed like several hours, he woke up to someone pulling on his arm. "Dominick, Dominick. Jamie is crying."

Dominick rolled out of bed and stumbled toward the sound of sobbing. "What's the matter, Jamie?"

Jamie's voice was muffled by the sleeping bag.

"What? Pull the covers off your head so I can hear you."

"I have to go to the bathroom and I'm scared to go outside," Jamie gasped.

"Why? You know the way and there's nothing to be afraid of."

"Yes there is. The 'Lonely One' that you told us about." His voice was defensive and louder.

"Shh. That was just a story, it's not real." Dominick chuckled at the idea that Jamie was still scared. He thought that was a credit to his storytelling ability.

"But that's not what you told us. He's real, and I don't want to go out there. Will you go with me?" he whined.

"You don't need me. Just run over there and get it over with."

"NO! I won't go by myself. I'm going to stand on the porch and pee out the door." Jamie was yelling now. The other boys were sleepily complaining about being awakened.

"All right, all right. I'll walk with you. Geez..." Dominick pulled on his sweatshirt, shorts, and sandals for the short walk across the commons. Jamie clung to him all the way over and all the way back; when they returned, he made a dash for his bed. Dominick went back to sleep without undressing and woke up in the morning feeling tired and unprepared for the day.

Most of that day Jamie was quiet and unenthusiastic, even about his visit to the snack shop, which he usually loved. Dominick assumed that the boy, like himself, was tired from lack of sleep.

That night, as the boys were getting ready for bed, Jamie was standing by the cabin door and bouncing from one leg to the other.

"What's the matter, Jamie?" asked Dominick.

"I'm waiting for someone to go to the bathroom with me. It's dark, and the Lonely One might be out there!"

The other boys laughed, but Dominick didn't think that Jamie was trying to be funny. Without saying anything, he walked through the door, with Jamie following very closely. "I don't understand, Jamie. Seriously, are you still scared by my story?"

"Yeah, man, it scared the 'you-know-what' out of me."

"But it's not real. It's just a story." As he said it, Dominick realized that this argument probably was not effective.

"That doesn't make any difference, it's still scary." He turned toward Dominick, waiting for him to respond.

4. A Contest of Wills

"What's for dinner tonight, Alice?" asked eleven-year-old Erin of her counselor as the girls seated themselves in the dining hall. "I'm hungry." Erin was one of the more active, energetic girls in the group. She was usually cheerful but was sometimes inclined to be moody.

"I don't know, Erin," Alice said. "We'll see in a few minutes, though. I'm ready for a big meal, too."

The main course turned out to be sauerkraut and bratwurst. "Oh no, not sauerkraut," Erin said. Each of the other girls took some, even though it was not their favorite. Before taking her own, Alice offered some to Erin, who was sitting next to her.

"Okay!" Erin said brightly, but with obvious sarcasm. "This ought to be fun." She took a "brat" and scooped some sauerkraut, making her distaste apparent.

"Why did you take it if you don't like it?" asked Alice. "You know the rules. You don't have to take it, but if you do, you'd better eat it."

"Kraut can be fun, if you drop it like this," said Erin as she flipped a forkful onto the table, making a satisfying splat. "Isn't that great?" The other girls rewarded her with a laugh.

Alice calmly cleaned it up. "All right, you've had your fun. Now you can just settle down and eat the rest!"

"I'm not going to eat this junk," replied Erin grimly. "I can't stand it!"

Alice began to get annoyed. "Look," she said, "you took the food, you eat it. Food is not a toy!"

"I said I'm not going to eat it and I'm not!"

"She's going to sit here until she eats it," muttered Alice to no one in particular. Before long, the group was ready for dessert, but Erin was still sitting in silence, glaring at her plate.

Alice saved a brownie for her, while the others ate theirs. When they were finished, Alice again asked Erin to try the sauerkraut. By now it was cold and mushy. Erin refused again. "You're going to sit here until you eat it!" Alice said. "I don't care if it takes the rest of the summer. And we'll sit here with you." The other girls groaned and began to urge Erin to give in so that they could leave. Alice had counted on that but was not prepared for Erin's reaction. Erin became even more defiant than before, and it was evident that the pressure was stiffening her resistance. Realizing this, the other campers asked Alice to let them go, pleading that it wasn't fair to punish them, too.

Seeing that the situation was rapidly getting worse instead of better, Alice dismissed the group, and she and Erin remained seated at the table alone. Erin ignored her. Twenty minutes later they were still there. The kitchen staff wanted to close up for the night, and Alice was due at the campfire site to prepare the evening program.

5. It Takes Two to Tangle

Toby, one of the most conscientious of the new counselors, came into the head counselor's office sputtering and waving his arms. It did not take much insight to tell John, the head counselor, that the young man was angry. This was not the first time that Toby had come to him with a problem, nor was he surprised to see Toby so upset. John leaned back in his chair and motioned to another chair near the desk. "What's up?"

Toby slapped his hands on his knees and sighed, "It's that Sanders kid again. That little punk should be sent home. He's a bad influence on the rest of the guys. They won't listen to me. Him they listen to! Me they laugh at. And it's all because he tells them to!"

John leaned forward. "Tells them to what, Toby?"

"Well, he was smoking in the cabin again. I caught him and told him he couldn't get away with that in *my* cabin. I told him he couldn't go on the hike today, and I wasn't going to let him go to the movie tonight, either. I made an example of him for the others to see. Right in front of all his buddies, I told him that no punk twelve-year-old kid was going to break the rules and get away with it. I told him plenty. He didn't say a word. Nobody said a thing. I thought I had everything under control."

John encouraged him to continue. "Then what happened, Toby?"

"I'll tell you what happened! When it was time for the boys to have their rest period, they all just sat on their bunks. I told them to lie down, and they didn't say a word — they just sat there. Well, I'm no dope. I knew who was behind it. I went to Sanders and told him to cut out the nonsense. He just smiled at me. I told him it was going to be him or me. He laughed at me and said something under his breath. It sounded like a dirty name. I told him to get out. He got up and walked to the door and sat outside. The other kids just acted like I wasn't there! I wasn't going to stand for that, so I walked out. Jim, from the next cabin, is watching them now."

The head counselor looked at Toby. John had been trying since the beginning of the season to find a way to help him overcome his excitability. There had been problems before, but Toby had never appeared quite so disorganized or overwhelmed. Yet it was true that Bobby Sanders was a youngster with serious problems, and quite capable of disrupting even a well-organized group. He had been accepted at camp with serious reservations. John finally took a deep breath and said, "What do you think about it, Toby? Where do we go from here?"

6. Like Night and Day

"I always have this problem," sobbed Patty. "Whenever I'm away from home, I get scared and lonely. Especially at night. I just don't know what to do!" Three days had passed since the campers arrived and Patty was still having trouble. Her counselor had taken her for a walk to try to sort things out. "It's just me," Patty continued. "The kids are great, I love camp, and I know you're doing all you can to help me."

"Do you have any idea why you have this trouble?" Mary Anne asked the ten-year-old. "You've made a lot of friends, and everybody likes you."

"I don't know," Patty replied. "Every day, I tell myself it won't happen again, and I'm fine until bedtime. But then I get lonely and start to cry, and I can't fall asleep."

Mary Anne was also at a loss. She had noticed the problem the first night and given Patty some extra attention, but the girl had still cried herself to sleep. The next night, Mary Anne had let the girls stay up long after lights out to talk with her, and they were all sympathetic and tried to help. Just last night, Patty had been permitted to call home before she went to bed, but that hadn't helped, either.

"Do you feel like you want to go home?" asked Mary Anne, wanting to understand all she could and not knowing what else to say.

"No, I like it here," shrugged Patty. "But I want to stop feeling bad."

"We're trying everything we know," said Mary Anne. "And be sure to tell us if you have any other ideas. Would it help for you to tell yourself that you'll try not to get too homesick just for tonight, and try to think of the fun you'll have tomorrow?"

"Okay, I'll try. I'll try anything!" Patty smiled for the first time since they had started their walk.

"We're here for you, Patty," nodded Mary Anne as they approached the cabin.

At bedtime that night, Mary Anne noticed that Patty was still having trouble and sat down on the edge of the girl's bed. Patty suddenly broke into tears. "It's no use," she sobbed. "I can't do it. Maybe you're right. Maybe I should just go home and try to forget about the whole thing!"

7. It's Not Fair

Nine-year-old Angela was busy packing her suitcase. "What are you doing?" asked Sheila, her counselor.

"I'm leaving."

"What do you mean, 'leaving'? You aren't supposed to go home until Saturday, and it's only Wednesday."

"So what? I'm finished with this place now, and I'm going home," insisted Angela, who was normally an easygoing child with a cheerful disposition.

"But I don't understand. You've been having fun, haven't you? Why would things change now?" Sheila was baffled.

"Things have just changed, that's all." Angela picked up her suitcase and headed out the door. Sheila followed at a respectful distance as Angela started towards the gate, heavy suitcase in hand. *Why is she doing this?* Sheila wondered, and she hoped to get Angela to volunteer the information. She didn't want to try to force Angela to do anything.

After walking and dragging the suitcase for about a quarter of a mile, Angela stopped to rest. Sitting on her suitcase, she watched as Sheila approached. Neither of them spoke, and Sheila sat down in the grass by the side of the road.

After a few moments, Angela stood up and picked up the suitcase, apparently ready to go on. "Can I carry that for you for a while?" asked Sheila. Silently, Angela set it down and watched Sheila pick it up and start down the road.

"This thing is going to get awfully heavy by the time we get to town," Sheila added, "and we're going to get pretty tired, since it'll probably take hours to get there. Do you want to talk about it?"

Angela's face was grim as she continued down the road. "I've had enough of camp. It hasn't been any fun; I miss my Mom; I'm tired of the food; Jennifer gets all the attention." Angela's statements came quickly but without much emotion.

"But I thought you've been having a good time," Sheila responded. "I can understand why you miss home, but you'll be going there in three days anyway. In a couple of weeks, you'll be bored at home and wish you were at camp. The food isn't always the greatest, I agree, but usually it's okay." Sheila paused and thought about the rest of Angela's statement. "What do you mean Jennifer gets all the attention?"

Jennifer was another girl in Sheila's group. She was very different from Angela; she was a constant challenge and demanded intense personal attention. Sheila was proud of the way she had worked with Jennifer and felt satisfied with her apparent progress.

"Jennifer's always doing something to get attention and you're always giving it to her. The rest of us don't do anything and we get ignored most of the time. It's not fair."

Sheila's heart sank as Angela's meaning became clear. Angela was right. She *had* been focusing her attention on Jennifer almost to the exclusion of the others, who seemed to need so much less from her. Apparently that exclusion had not gone unnoticed, and perhaps the other girls needed her more than she had realized. Now Angela was waiting for her to respond.

8. The Acid Test

"Matt, Matt, guess what!" shouted Dan as he ran excitedly into the cabin. "I just passed my swimming test!"

Matt, his counselor, was very pleased and got up to give him a congratulatory hug. "That's great, Dan. It's a real accomplishment, something to be proud of." A few years before, when Matt was still a senior camper, Dan had come to camp for the first time. Matt remembered that for the first few weeks, Dan had been so terrified of the water that he wouldn't even go near the edge. Some of the senior boys, Matt among them, had taken an interest in him and had gradually helped him to overcome some of his fear. Dan had learned to swim the next summer and now had passed his advanced swimming test. Indeed, Matt could genuinely share his feeling of accomplishment. He made a mental note to tell the story to Lance, the swimming instructor, who was new at camp and probably didn't know about Dan's history.

"That's not an easy test, Dan," Matt added. "I want you to know that it takes a very strong swimmer to be able to pass. You've come a long way. You have to swim a hundred yards of each of the major strokes, don't you, in addition to the other parts of the test?"

Dan grinned sheepishly. "Actually, we didn't take that part of the test," he said. "Lance said he didn't have the time, so as long as we knew the strokes, that's all he cared about. He knows that some of us can't swim that far, but he passed us anyway. Wasn't that nice of him?"

9. Fact or Fiction?

Marcus had started the fourth session of camp well rested and anticipating a good week. In this, his first summer, he had moved from nervousness at the beginning of the season to his present confidence that he possessed the skills and maturity to be a responsible and effective cabin counselor.

Today, the third day of the session, was sunny and not too warm. He and his group had just returned from the archery range and were getting seated in the dining hall. Edie, the camp director, passed their table. "Marcus, can you stop by the office on your way back from dinner?" she asked. "I have something I need to ask you about."

"Sure, that would be fine. I'll ask Aaron to walk back with my kids while I'm there."

After dinner, Marcus dropped some mail in the box located near the main office and walked in. "Marcus," Edie said, after he had gotten seated, "Corey talked to me this afternoon and complained that some of the other boys in your cabin are stealing from him and that you aren't doing anything about it. He would like to know what's going on."

"Well, Corey has been accusing others of stealing, but we usually find what he's looking for in the bottom of his suitcase or lying around the cabin. Corey is careless and very quick to accuse others to cover for his mistakes."

"Is there anything he hasn't found?"

"We've been looking for a gold-colored chain necklace he says that he brought with him."

"Corey says that one of the other campers has his chain and won't give it back."

"I haven't seen it, and the other kids say they haven't either. He hasn't accused anyone specifically, and we don't look through campers' things without permission. The last time something was missing, his towel, he accused Terry of stealing it. Terry gave us permission to look in his suitcase and it wasn't there. Eventually we found it in the 'lost and found' at the beach."

"I'll talk to him about it," Edie responded, "and I'll suggest some things he should do before accusing others. But will you help him to take better care of his stuff?"

"Sure." Marcus walked out of the office toward his cabin. As he approached, he saw Corey walking determinedly in his direction. "Marcus, I'm sure Chad has my gold necklace. Can you check his suitcase? It has to be there."

10. For Love or Money?

The night seemed hushed and still in contrast to the rapid tempo of the activities of the day. The four adults who sat in the office drinking coffee were tired and concerned. Diane, the camp director, finally spoke. "Let's go over the facts again. Tell us just what happened, Tom."

Tom, a twenty-four-year-old college graduate and an experienced counselor, replied, "I got back from town at 9:45 yesterday morning, just in time to join my group for the 10 o'clock swim. I had withdrawn $25 dollars from the cash machine and put the money in my wallet. The wallet was in the pocket of my trousers. I hung them up in the cabin when I put on my bathing suit. After the swim, I took out my wallet so that I could put the money away in a safer place, and I found that the two ten-dollar bills and the five-dollar bill were missing. I didn't mention it to you, Diane, until about an hour later, after I had looked through my pockets and around the cabin area. I thought that was the last I'd see of the money, and it was really my own fault for being so careless. But I didn't think anyone in camp would do a thing like this."

"Unfortunately, we can never be sure," replied Diane, the camp director. "I thought that was the end of the money too, Tom, until Kevin appeared with it near the end of rest period. Just how did you come across it, Kevin?"

Kevin, Tom's supervisor, frowned as he told his story. "I was hoping to check in with Tom and was thinking about this incident. While walking through the cabin, I noticed some money sticking out over the edge of Johnny Green's lower shelf, under his shirts. You're probably thinking, just as I did, that it was all too simple. Anyone who had the nerve to take money from a counselor's wallet would surely hide it more carefully than that. However, I looked, and sure enough, it was the same amount that Tom had reported missing. I hesitated, but I finally decided to take the money. I gave it to Tom outside the cabin. That's about all, I think."

"What are your impressions of Johnny, Tom?" asked Diane.

Tom thought for a minute before he spoke. "He's a quiet, likable kid, and he's a little shy about participating in most of the activities. He needs a great deal of encouragement. About the only thing he really looks forward to is mealtime."

"That fits with what I've seen," said Kevin. "I have the feeling that the regularity of our mealtimes and the rest of the schedule is very important to him. This is probably the first time in his life he has had the security of knowing what to expect, and when. He seems to be enjoying camp and gaining a great deal from it. That's a real tribute to you, Tom."

"This matter has not been mentioned to Johnny at all yet," said Diane. "In fact, we don't know for sure that he's the one who took the money. How do you think we should deal with it?"

11. On the Home Front

Danielle, a ten-year-old camper in Erica's cabin, was refusing to put on her bathing suit. This was the third day in a row that she had not gone swimming, and she had not done much of anything else either, although she had been one of the most active and enthusiastic of all the campers the year before. Her cabinmates, after repeatedly inviting her but getting no response, eventually began to ignore her. Erica had not found Danielle to be a serious behavior problem, but she was worried about her.

"Danielle, why don't you try it just once? You'll enjoy the cool water on such a hot day," said Erica.

"I don't think so," sighed Danielle.

"But you haven't gone yet and, if you go home without swimming this year, you'll regret it later."

"I don't care!" Danielle's tone was firmer.

"Of course you care. Here, let me help you find your bathing suit." Erica started to open Danielle's suitcase.

"No! I don't want to," Danielle cried as she jumped on the suitcase. "If you make me I'll run away!"

Perplexed, Erica said, "I don't understand. What's wrong?"

"Nothing. My parents are getting a divorce and sent me to camp to get me out of the house and I just don't feel like it, okay? Just leave me alone." Danielle lay down on her bed and turned her head toward the wall.

12. I Wanna Hold Your Hand

The boys were traipsing down the sunlit lakeside path on their way to lunch. They had spent the morning working on the catapult, which they hoped to have built by the last day of camp. Keith, their counselor, was feeling content and even proud. They had worked hard all morning, and most of the afternoon was going to be spent in water sports, an easy activity for Keith.

Walking together accordion style, the boys were roughhousing with each other and with Keith. As they approached the dining hall, Drew ran up behind Keith, jumped up onto his back, slid down to the ground, and grabbed his hand. Moving around to Keith's side, he walked hand-in-hand with Keith for a few strides.

Keith was immediately uncomfortable with the idea of a thirteen-year-old holding his hand. "Hey," he bellowed as he jerked his hand away. "What are you doing? Are you gay or something?"

Drew blushed, and the other boys yelled in derision. Keith realized that he had reacted too quickly and thoughtlessly.

That afternoon Drew kept his distance from Keith; usually, they were never far apart, as Drew always sought Keith's attention. Now, though, the boy was obviously avoiding him. The other boys had not forgotten the morning's incident.

"Gay boy."

"Drew likes boys."

"Fem."

This is my fault, thought Keith, but what can I do to correct it?

13. Misplaced Trust

Derrick's ten-year-old boys had been telling "Can you top this?" stories all afternoon while they waited for the rain to stop. They were sprawled around on their bunks and on the floor. When the conversation lagged, Derrick asked, "What's the worst thing that ever happened to you?"

"In school I had a locker in the same locker room with all the football players. Every day when I'd go to change they would snap me with their towels and give me wedgies." Everyone laughed ruefully. They could see the pain in Mario's face.

"My parents left me at a rest stop on the freeway once!" Ian exclaimed.

"What? Are you for real?"

"Yeah, I was six years old and we were on vacation. It's like, I have four brothers and sisters and, when it was time to go, everyone piled into the van and no one counted to make sure we were all there. I was still in the bathroom."

"How long did they leave you for? What did you do?"

"I don't know. It seemed like three hours. I was crying and yelling for them to come back. Some lady saw me and asked me my name and hunted around for my parents, but we couldn't find them. So she called the police."

"Really!"

"Yeah, but my parents came back about the same time the cop came. I was really happy to see them. They felt so bad, they bought me a biiiiiig ice cream cone and were really nice to me the rest of the day. My brothers and sisters were so jealous."

"But weren't you scared?"

"Yeah. I thought I was going to get kidnapped and molested! You know how the rest stop has posters of missing children who've been kidnapped and everything."

Conner was next. "I was bitten by a Doberman. I was walking down the street with my brother and this dog came running around the corner of a house. I was so scared, I couldn't move!"

"So what did you do?"

"Nothing, like I said, I was scared and I couldn't move and the dog was so fast. Anyway, there's no way I could run faster than him. So he ran right up to me and I screamed and he bit me on the leg. Then his owner came out and called him away. I was so glad he was gone, and I was crying. I turned around and looked for my brother and he wasn't there. He was so scared that he ran away!"

There was a pause, and then Bobby said quietly, "I was molested."

Derrick looked up. "What do you mean?"

"Well, my neighbor used to invite me over to his house to watch cable, and one day he made me put his penis in my mouth."

"Oh, man, that's sick," said Conner.

"Yeah, why'd you have to tell us that?"

As Bobby suddenly looked ashamed, Derrick cleared his throat.

14. For the Sake of Appearances

Ronnie was one of a small number of African Americans campers, and one of the best liked and most highly respected campers of all. He was always willing to teach others the skills he had long since mastered, and he managed to be friends with many different types of people. Marie was surprised, therefore, when some of her fourteen-year-old girls came to her, apparently worried, to report that one of their cabinmates, Tara, was spending a lot of her spare time with him.

"Don't all of you spend a lot of time talking with Ronnie?" she asked. "He goes to Tara's high school and they're both interested in literature, so I guess they have a lot in common." She knew what the girls really meant, but she chose to let them say it directly if they would.

"You don't understand, Marie," said one. "We think they like each other, like boyfriend and girlfriend. We've talked to her, but it hasn't done any good. She says they just enjoy talking together, and that's all there is to it. But we think you should break it up before she gets too involved."

"Even if I wanted to break it up," asked Marie, "how would you suggest I go about it? What do you think would happen if I just told her to stop being seen with him?"

They got the point. "Then maybe you should talk to the director," someone said, "and have him tell Ronnie to cut it out."

Marie was beginning to get angry. "Cut what out?" she asked. "What have they done wrong?"

"Well," said Melody, who seemed to be the leader of the delegation, "we don't want to have anything to do with her."

Marie exploded. "What you're saying is cruel! It's one thing if you're trying to protect Tara and Ronnie from developing a relationship that society may make painful for them later. But now you're saying that if Tara likes Ronnie, you have no interest in being her friend any more. That's true friendship, isn't it? Maybe she's smarter than you think. Ronnie seems to be a much worthier friend than any of you are. Anyway, I wouldn't be surprised if you're a little jealous."

Tight-lipped, the girls walked away. Those girls will realize what's right when they cool off, she thought. She, too, had noticed how much time Tara and Ronnie had been spending together. It had not particularly concerned her, but in view of the girls' reaction, Marie thought she had better speak with Tara.

Marie managed to take a walk with Tara alone that evening. "Tara, some of the girls have been talking about your relationship with Ronnie," she said.

"Yes, I know," said Tara. "They want me to keep away from him, and some of them have been pretty nasty about it. It's none of their business, is it? What right do they have to butt in?"

"No right at all, unless they were genuinely concerned for a friend's welfare — yours or Ronnie's," answered Marie. "And judging from the way they spoke to me, I doubt if that's the case. Anyway, I'm always available if you want to talk. You know that."

Marie heard little more of the matter for several days until one afternoon just after the mail had been distributed. Tara suddenly looked up from the letter she was reading, gasped, and ran out of the cabin, tears streaming down her face. Marie followed her, and together they walked down to the edge of the lake. Gradually, Tara's crying subsided and she was able to speak.

"It's from my mother," she said. "Someone told her that I was going with Ronnie. She writes that if I don't keep completely away from him, she's going to take me home. She doesn't even want me to be seen talking to him! She could at least ask me if it's true. She just doesn't trust me. All she cares about is how it looks to other people. Who do you think told her a thing like that, Marie?"

"I got a letter from your mother today too, Tara," Marie said, "but I was reading another one first when you ran out. I didn't dream it was about this. I'll get it and come right back." Marie walked quickly back to the cabin and got the letter, while fending off the curious questions from the other girls in the group. She opened it as she walked back toward the lake and began to read.

Dear Marie,

This morning, Mrs. Anderson (she's Melody's mother and a friend of mine) showed me a letter from Melody that said Tara is very friendly with a black camper. You know the problems this can cause, so I want all contact between them stopped immediately. If the boy cannot be convinced to stay away, he should be sent home. I'm not prejudiced, but I don't approve of interracial dating. I'm sure you understand. Please notify me promptly that this matter has been taken care of.
   Tara seems very happy at camp, for which I thank you.

Sincerely yours,
Mrs. John Ellwood

Tara met her on the path before she reached the lake. "What did she say, Marie?" asked the girl, with a sad and worried expression on her face.

15. Where Do We Go from Here?

Ever since she was hired, Laura had been looking forward to the camp season with special anticipation. The camp program was focused on social responsibility and service based on a religious commitment, exactly what she felt that organized camping should be about.

Now that the season had begun, she was bursting with excitement. One of the new campers in her group, Christy, was a special source of joy, reminding Laura of herself a few years earlier. Christy couldn't stop talking about how much she was looking forward to the summer, with the opportunities it promised for her to make a difference in the world. In particular, she was looking forward to the chance to help some of the poverty-stricken families who lived not far away.

Christy's family lived in an exclusive neighborhood and had little interest in and less contact with the problems of the rest of the world. Most of her classmates led similarly sheltered lives, and Christy had confided to Laura how excited she was about the opportunity to make new friends at camp who shared her interests and commitment.

A few days later, however, Laura was taken by surprise when she walked into the cabin and found Christy alone, sitting on her bed, apparently near tears. "Hey, why so glum?" asked Laura.

"To be honest," responded Christy, "I'm thinking about leaving."

Laura tried to hide her surprise. "I'm sorry that I didn't realize that there were problems," she said. "You seemed so happy. What happened?"

"There's no way you could have known. I can put up a good front, and I have been having fun, but ... it's just not what I expected."

"How?"

"I guess I thought the kids would be different. Do you remember how I told you how excited I was to be at camp with kids whose values are more like mine?" Laura nodded quietly as she listened. "Well, it's not happening," Christy continued. "I think I'm more serious about it than they are. They're good kids and all, but they're not so different from the ones back home. Do you think I'm expecting too much?"

"And that's why you want to leave?"

"Yeah."

"I think that would be sad. There is so much that people could learn from you — your attitudes, your commitment to what we stand for here, things like that. Let me ask you another question. Have you found any role models here at all, anyone who represents what you were looking for?"

"Of course! You, for example! And some of the other counselors, and the chaplain. And some of the older kids, too."

"Have you learned anything from them?"

"Sure! Lots!"

"Well, I think that's a major accomplishment, something to be excited about. And the friends you've made. It's important to look at the positives before you make a decision like leaving camp."

"I don't know. I'll have to think about it," replied Laura as she stood up from her bed. "I'm just as lonely here most of the time as I am at home, and I don't know what to do."

16. Disability Equals Dumb?

Maria was watching Carmen, one of her fourteen-year-old campers, who was leaning on the gate to the swimming area looking sad and lonely. Maria thought that Carmen really was lonely. All the girls in the cabin had come to the beach as a group but, as usual, Carmen was the last to be chosen as a buddy for swimming, and she showed no interest in going into the water. Maria had seen Carmen's spirit deflate like a balloon two days after the party.

Carmen had a speech disability as a result of a car accident when she was younger. She talked slowly, was hard to understand, and had difficulty getting words out. Unfortunately, her disability made it easy for others to conclude that her intelligence was also impaired, and the girls, while not trying to be mean, routinely acted as if she was not able to participate intelligently in camp life.

Just yesterday, they had been trying to figure out how to solve an orienteering problem. The girls had not planned properly and had become lost. But it could have been avoided, because Maria had heard Carmen try to warn them about their choice. No one bothered to listen to her. It was obvious to Maria that Carmen probably understood orienteering better than most, perhaps having learned to listen carefully to instructions because it was hard for her to ask questions.

Even if Carmen *were* mentally impaired, Maria thought, it still wouldn't be right for them to treat her like this. But if I say anything, she'll feel even more singled out and embarrassed. If I don't intervene, she'll continue to have a bad time and be lonely. Maria sighed.

These thoughts were interrupted by a sound nearby, and she looked up to find Carmen approaching. "Hi Marie," she said haltingly. "Can I go back to the cabin? I'm not having any fun here."

17. Hurling Hailey

"Renee! Hailey is throwing up again," Jodi said as she came running from the showerhouse.

"Again?" Renee asked. "Did she throw up before? This is the first I've heard of it."

"She threw up last night, too," Jodi replied.

"I'll check on her. You girls go on to arts and crafts, and I'll meet you there." Renee headed toward the showerhouse.

Just as she arrived, Hailey opened the door and walked out. A pleasant, attractive fourteen year old who usually dressed meticulously, Hailey nonetheless usually kept to herself and appeared to have few friends. "Are you okay?" Renee asked.

"I'm fine," Hailey replied.

"Jodi said you were throwing up just now and that you did last night, too."

"Oh, sometimes my stomach gets upset if I eat the wrong things. It's happened before. It's no big deal."

"Maybe you should go see the nurse anyway."

"No, I don't want to do that. I'll be fine."

Renee did not pursue it any further, but she decided to keep a close eye on Hailey. A few days passed and Hailey seemed to be fine. She was apparently eating normally, she bought snacks at the canteen every afternoon, and she was participating in various activities. Renee thought that whatever was wrong had passed. Eventually she forgot about it, having many other things on her mind, such as what they were going to do for talent night.

A week later, Jodi again mentioned to Renee that she had heard Hailey throwing up. Jodi had returned to the cabin to get her notebook when she heard Hailey in the bathroom all by herself. Renee realized that the problem might be more serious than she had thought, so she decided to talk to Amy, the nurse, about it.

"She says that she's fine, and she didn't want to come to see you about it," Renee explained. "By the way, please don't tell her that I did — I'll do that myself at the right time. Could there be something going on that I don't know about?"

Amy agreed that more was probably going on with Hailey than she was letting on. "Her throwing up is not normal. It sounds to me like some kind of bulimia, which is often the result of emotional or self-image problems. Whatever the reason, she may need some help. I'll try to keep an eye her, and be sure to let me know if the problem continues so we can check out any other medical possibilities. Meanwhile, see what you can do to get her to come out of herself and to be more involved with the other girls. She needs to experience as much success as she can. That's where camp can really make a difference for her."

As she walked back toward the cabin, Renee realized perhaps for the first time how important her job as a counselor was, and she pondered how she might best be able to be helpful.

Working with Campers in Groups

18. A Case of Chaos

Travis was thinking about his first three days as a counselor as he walked slowly toward his cabin after breakfast. The campers had arrived on Sunday, and he could hardly believe that it was Wednesday morning already. Yet he felt as if he had known the boys in his group for a long time. Most of them had been at camp before, and he sensed that they enjoyed his own unfamiliarity with camp life.

He shook his head and grinned, remembering the excitability of eight year olds and how easily they seemed to "catch" moods from one another. But he was worried about George, a new camper, very small and shy, who seemed to have become the scapegoat of the group. It was time, Travis decided, to seek the advice of the head counselor about him.

Still about thirty yards from his cabin, Travis suddenly became aware of loud noises coming from that direction. He had already learned that the unusually high-pitched voices he heard meant that something was up. This was surprising to him, since he thought the cabin cleanup routine following breakfast had been clearly established by his careful attention to it on the previous two mornings. In fact, Travis was pleased at the discipline he had been able to establish by being very strict for the first few days — "to show them who's boss." He planned to ease up as soon as he felt the campers were ready for it.

He broke into a trot that carried him to the door of the cabin in a few seconds, and he looked inside to see Dominic and Karl throwing clothes at each other, screaming with glee. In the middle of the floor, two campers with brooms were angrily sweeping each other's feet. A pillow flew between them, thrown by Tony, who was jumping up and down on his bed, yelling. His attention attracted by George's cries of pain, Travis saw two other boys taunting and hitting him. Some of the beds were overturned, including Travis's own, and everyone's belongings were strewn around the floor. He wondered how so much excitement could have been generated and so much damage done in the few minutes since they had all left the dining hall together, when the campers had run up to the cabin ahead of him.

Momentarily stunned by the scene of utter chaos, Travis quickly recovered and loudly slammed the door, hoping that the sudden noise would distract the campers long enough for him to gain control. But they seemed not to hear, so he moved rapidly toward George, who seemed to be in some immediate danger of physical injury. When George was separated from his tormentors, Travis turned to the others and tried to get them to calm down, his own tension level rising all the time. Their excitement still at a fever pitch, the two campers he had separated from George began calling the boy a crybaby and throwing shoes at him. With a scream of desperation, George stood up and tore wildly out of the cabin. Out of the corner of his eye, Travis saw him running full speed across the path and into the woods.

Fully conscious of his first responsibility to keep his campers safe, Travis knew that no young camper, especially one in George's condition, should be roaming the woods alone. It was also obvious that the boy was deeply upset and in need of help and comfort. But the mood of the group had risen to a high pitch, and physical danger was involved there as well. No other adult was within hearing distance to be called to help, since the other two cabin groups based in the immediate area were away on an early morning hike and breakfast cookout. Pausing momentarily at the door of the cabin, Travis could feel himself trembling as George disappeared from sight over the hill among the trees.

19. The Squeaky Wheel Gets the Grease

George was leading a discussion with the boys in his group, and it wasn't going so well. As hard as he tried, there were a few boys who seemed to be out of control as usual. Every time the discussion started moving, one of them would crack a joke or find some other way to disrupt the flow.

Fed up and feeling unproductive, George finally decided to negotiate. "Hold it, guys, I see you're a little jumpy, so let's try this. How about we pay attention for the next fifteen minutes and then I'll let you go fifteen minutes early." He noticed that the "trouble-makers" seemed to be satisfied but the others were quieter. Overall, however, he concluded that the consensus of the group was with him.

The next fifteen minutes proved to be more productive, particularly because the noisy ones who had not participated before were now as active as the others in the discussion. Fifteen minutes later, Jimmy, the leader of the loud kids, abruptly popped up and said, "That's your fifteen minutes! Time to go."

Although the discussion was going well and had just begun to get to the crucial issues, George knew he had no choice. "Okay, a deal's a deal," he said. "I hope the next time we can get going from the start. I'll see you guys later."

At this point, most of the boys jumped up and ran out, but as George was getting his things together, he noticed that some of the quieter ones were still hanging around. "What's doing, guys?" he asked. "Don't you want to go play some ball?"

"Yeah, I guess we will," responded Chad. "But we just don't understand why you always go along with them and we never get to do what we want. Why should they be able make the discussion end before the end of the period just when it starts to get good?"

20. *"The Best Laid Plans…"*

"Thanks for your suggestions," said Rochelle to her supervisor, Bobbie. "I'll do my best."

They had just finished discussing the one major problem that Rochelle felt was standing in the way of an unusually happy and constructive summer experience for her group of twelve-year-old girls. Their spirit was good, and they participated with enthusiasm in a variety of camp activities. Rochelle was concerned, however, about their cliquishness. Except for the only new camper in the group, all had been cabinmates the summer before, and many were neighbors at home. They continually made it clear that they did not want Marcia, nor any other campers for that matter, to join in their activities and share their fun. Rochelle had made several attempts to help them broaden their perspective, but she had been rebuffed each time.

Marcia was a pleasant and rather quiet girl, but camp life was a totally new experience for her. She seemed to be having fun even though she had not been accepted by her cabinmates. Although they did not actively dislike her, she was the butt of most of their pranks. Rochelle felt that the situation was unhealthy not only for Marcia, but also for the other girls, who were using her as a scapegoat.

Mattie seemed to be the most influential camper in the group, and her leadership was usually directed toward sound, positive objectives. The others followed her with little question or reservation and usually with good results. But Rochelle was disturbed by the fact that Mattie seemed to promote the exclusion of Marcia and other campers from the "in-group." These observations had led Rochelle to ask Bobbie for her suggestions.

Bobbie had pointed out several possible explanations of the situation and various ways in which Rochelle might try to handle it. She agreed with Rochelle that something should be done, adding that "it's a sign that something's wrong when a group becomes exclusive and self-centered, no matter how good its spirit may seem in other ways."

Rochelle had still not decided how she would approach the problem. She wondered whether to work directly with Mattie or with the group as a whole. She thought it might be best not to involve

Marcia directly, especially since the issue was really more general in scope, but realized that this would be difficult. Whatever she was going to do, Rochelle decided, it was important for her to choose the time carefully. Fortunately, the group had planned a cookout and campfire for that evening, and Rochelle thought there might be an opportunity then. After dinner, when the girls were sitting quietly around a crackling fire at twilight, was usually a good time for discussions. She would wait until then and would try to plan an effective approach in the meantime.

The day passed quickly, and by midafternoon the girls had picked up their food and equipment at the kitchen and started out for the campfire site. They went to an area about a quarter of a mile back in the woods, one they had prepared for themselves during the first week of camp. They were well organized, and before long the fire had been built, extra wood gathered, and the food prepared for cooking.

As usual, Mattie took the lead, and she began to throw the potatoes into the hot coals at the bottom of the fire. It was a breezy day and the smoke seemed to blow into Mattie's face no matter where she stood. She couldn't get very close, and several of the potatoes missed the fire completely. Some of the other girls noticed, and they began to laugh at her. Suddenly, she stood up with a smile on her face and said, "Marcia, will you do me a favor?"

Marcia looked up, surprised and pleased, and came over quickly from where she was piling firewood nearby. "Sure!" she said. "What do you want?"

"Will you go back to camp and ask Bobbie if we can borrow the smoke shifter?" asked Mattie. Marcia hesitated momentarily and looked around at the other girls, who tried to hide their snickers. Obviously not sure if she was the victim of another prank or not, she turned to Rochelle for some indication. Mattie caught Rochelle's eye and winked. Rochelle saw that the others were looking at her, too, their eyes begging her not to spoil their joke.

21. Democracy in Action?

"But *we* never get a chance to do what we want," protested Alex, speaking for Rico, Jerome, and himself. "We're always outvoted because the rest of the kids only want to play baseball."

"We take a fair vote every time," replied Marty. "That's the democratic way, isn't it? You're just not being a good sport about losing."

Their counselor, Deon, decided to listen for a while longer before speaking.

"Wouldn't it be fairer if you did what *we* want sometimes?" asked Alex.

"But democracy means majority rule," said Marty. "If you'd like to change things, then you should convince enough of us to switch our votes so that your side'll have the majority. Then we'll do what *you* want."

"Why can't Alex and Rico and I go to woodworking like we want to, and you guys do what you want to?" asked Jeremy.

Marty continued as spokesman for the majority. "That would be real nice," he said sarcastically. "It'd leave six of us to play baseball, and how much fun can you have playing baseball with six guys? You'd be spoiling it for the majority, and that's not fair or democratic."

"Well, is it fair or democratic for us not to get a chance to do what we like at all?" asked Alex.

Deon felt it was time for him to intervene. "First of all," he said, "group activity time is designed to be just that, a time for us to share an activity as a group. We all have a chance to do things individually and a chance to do things together. I think we should take advantage of both."

"Yes, but Jeremy and Alex and Rico won't cooperate," said Marty.

"We cooperate," replied Jeremy, "but why should we always have to do something we don't like?!"

Jeremy and Marty were beginning to get annoyed at each other. "Look, you're just a lousy sport!" said Marty. "You only want to do what you want to do, and to hell with the rest of the group."

"You're crazy!" was Jeremy's immediate retort. "I'll bet more than half these guys would enjoy woodworking just as much, but they're afraid to vote against you."

"Oh, Jeremy, stop being a baby!" responded Marty. "You lost fair and square."

Jeremy turned to the rest of the group. "You guys are cowards," he said. "Why don't you think for yourselves once in a while, instead of letting this dictator tell you what to do?"

Marty started to reply in kind, but Deon stepped in. "Guys, how about..."

22. Readiness, Leadership, and Democracy

Although she felt flattered, it was with real misgivings that Keri agreed to the director's request that she serve as staff adviser to the Campers' Council. "I'll help you as much as I can," the director, Helena, assured her, "but I'm sure you can handle it. You're the most experienced counselor on our staff, and I certainly don't know of anyone better qualified to interpret our point of view to the kids. Besides, you're skilled in democratic leadership, and that's the heart of the job."

"I think the Council should serve as a kind of camp parliament, representing the needs and interests of the kids and organizing all-camp projects and events," Keri replied, "but it always seems to become more of a 'gripe group,' where they bring their complaints and ask us — or even tell us — to do something about them. I'm not sure there's much educational value in that kind of thing, and the complaints can just as easily be made through the cabin counselors."

"I agree that often happens. It's hard to maintain the proper balance. In a way, I think the job of the adviser should be very much like running a cabin group," said Helena. "We want the kids to do as much planning and decisionmaking for themselves as possible, within the structure or framework provided by our rules and policies. Some camp policies and traditions change over time but, in general, not suddenly. Attention should usually be focused on the area within those limits. Of course, our Council also has the executive function of planning and carrying out its decisions."

"It seems to me that my job with the Council is as much one of leadership training as anything else, then," said Keri.

"Exactly! For example, it's very important that delegates learn that they have a responsibility to represent their cabinmates' opinions, not just their own. And there may be instances where a delegate has to choose between what seems best for his own group and what seems best for the camp as a whole. All these are teaching opportunities for you. This is why I chose you for this job," she said. "I firmly believe that there is a place for the kind of Campers' Council you favor, and I think you're the one who can develop it."

Thus, Keri found herself responsible for shifting the focus of attention and, in fact, the whole basic purpose of the Council. She decided to move slowly in changing basic concepts. As had been done in previous seasons, an announcement was made in the dining hall asking each cabin group to elect a Council representative. The first meeting was to be held the next day.

The meeting started smoothly. Most of the delegates had been at camp the year before and knew each other. Keri herself knew all but one or two. For the sake of the newcomers, however, she asked each girl to introduce herself briefly, and she held her own introduction until the end. Then she raised the question of the Council's purpose, hoping to get a group discussion started. "It gives us a way of telling the camp what we want," volunteered one of the older girls. The others seemed to agree.

Keri decided to try a new approach. "Yes," she said, "that's one of our purposes. But what are our responsibilities to camp and to the other campers?"

A long silence followed, broken by one of the older campers, Alisha. "Why don't we just get started?" she said. "Shouldn't we begin by electing officers?"

"I thought it might be better to wait until we know each other better," said Keri. "Could we pick a temporary chairperson, perhaps, and elect officers later?"

Again, Alisha was first to respond. "I was secretary last year, and none of the other former officers are here. Can I be the chair?" Keri saw the other campers nodding, and so she agreed. Alisha took over the meeting immediately. "Now, are there any issues we need to talk about?" she asked. There followed a long list of criticisms of the camp from various delegates including Alisha, all of which she duly listed on a sheet of paper.

"Tuesday's meal was gross." Everyone seemed to agree.

"They serve cheese too often." Here there seemed to be some

difference of opinion, and Keri addressed a question to the girl who had raised the issue.

"Is this the general opinion in your group or do you just hate cheese?" A little embarrassed, the girl confessed she was really expressing only a personal preference.

Keri assumed that the complaints would be discussed by the group, but when the list was complete, Alisha just handed it to her. "See what you can do about these things, will you, Keri?" she said. Then she turned back to the others. "Now shall we elect officers?"

"Wait a minute," interrupted Keri, suddenly deciding that the group might be lost completely unless she tried to redirect it now along the lines she and Helena had agreed upon. "First, I'd like to share with you some of my ideas about the purposes and responsibility of this Council. It's really supposed to be an instrument of self-government. She spoke for several minutes, covering all the points that she and Helena had discussed earlier. She placed special emphasis on the importance of camp rules, policies, and traditions as creating a framework within which the Council could exercise its responsibility.

"Fine!" said Alisha. "I have an idea for the Council to discuss. I propose that bedtime for each group should be an hour later than it is now. How do the delegates feel about it?" The group responded enthusiastically, and Alisha turned to Keri. "Well," she said, "everyone's certainly in favor of that. Can we do it?"

"We can discuss it," said Keri. But basically, I think that's an area in which the Council cannot make the final decision. It relates to your health, and the camp is responsible for that, so it's only fair that the camp should retain the power of decision."

"Well, then," said Alisha, "I think we might as well disband the Council. It's no different from what happens at home and at school. The adults say they want us to learn to plan and to govern ourselves, but when you come right down to it, they still insist on making all the real decisions."

23. Food for Thought

Kelly was proud of the way her eleven-year-old campers had worked together to plan their upcoming campout. She had tried to encourage them to participate in planning other things, but this was the first time they had really responded. Previously, they had preferred to let Kelly make the arrangements for whatever they did. When she had refused, saying that the responsibility should be shared, they had seemed content to pass the time not doing much of anything. That is, until the day before, when Marie had suggested an overnight. The others had all responded enthusiastically.

"I think that's a wonderful idea," Kelly said. "It certainly sounds like fun to me. When shall we go?" The girls asked her to find out when they could leave, and to make the necessary arrangements. "I think that's up to us," she replied. "As long as we give the kitchen a couple of days notice so they can have our food ready, we can leave just about whenever we want to. But I think it's our job to make the arrangements."

After a pause, Marie spoke up. "Kelly, whatever you arrange will be fine with us."

"I'm sorry, but I can't do it that way," Kelly answered. "I want us to go on the overnight and I'll be glad to help plan it, but I won't do it without your help. First of all, I don't think you're being fair, and I also feel that planning is an important part of the experience."

"Come on, Kelly," said Marie, "all you have to do is arrange the date and tell the kitchen, isn't it? I'll do it, if you'll come with me."

"There's more to it than that," replied Kelly. "What about menus, and how much of each item we'll need? Where are we going to sleep? What equipment and clothing should we take? What about the chores and the program? If we're going to use a prepared site, how do we know that it'll be vacant? There's a lot of planning to be done."

The girls acknowledged the point, and they began to work on the arrangements, food, and program. They planned the hike to begin three days later, on Thursday afternoon. They would use a popular camping site located on a peninsula at the far end of the lake and would return on Saturday morning. One of the girls went to the office to check on the site, found that it was available, and reserved it for the three days. They also began to list the equipment and clothing that they would need to take. The girls' enthusiasm increased markedly as they became more and more deeply involved.

Then they worked on the menus and the quantities of food that would be required. They were careful to plan meals that they could cook over an open fire and that would offer some degree of challenge. Edith and two other campers took the final copy to the kitchen so they could discuss it with Rose, the head cook, while Kelly and the rest of the group continued with the planning. Kelly was glad that the kitchen would have three days' notice instead of the required two; that made it more likely that all the requested food would be available.

A few minutes after she rejoined the discussion of travel plans, she noticed Edith and her two companions trudging dejectedly toward the cabin. She walked out onto the porch, where Edith was the first to see her. "Forget it, we can't go," said Edith.

"Why not?" asked Kelly. "What happened?"

"Rose said she has too many groups going out. She doesn't want any others for at least a week. Even then, she won't give us chicken like we asked for. She said we'll waste it because it'll spoil. And she said you should have come to her personally, instead of sending kids." The rest of the girls had gathered around, and as Edith finished, they walked silently back into the cabin. Kelly could tell that they were angry as well as disappointed. Fully aware of the potential impact of this incident on their attitudes and their spirit, she started slowly down the path toward the kitchen.

She could feel the annoyance rising in her as she walked, and she tried consciously to control it. Rose was standing near the door of the kitchen, and she spoke first. "Hi, Kelly. Some of your girls were just here asking something about food for a three-day trip starting Thursday, but I told them we couldn't do it. They really had an ambitious menu, too."

"I thought two days' notice is all we need to give you for something like this," replied Kelly. "We're not leaving for three days."

"Usually, two days is enough for us," Rose answered, "but there have just been too many groups going out recently, and we've had some other trouble in the kitchen. Give us a few days, and I'm sure we'll be able to help you."

Kelly tried to force herself to appear calm. "Rose, let me explain how important this is," she said. Kelly proceeded to tell her of the girls' general apathy and to relate how the hike had been planned and had stimulated so much enthusiasm. "Don't you see," she concluded, "if the kids are disappointed now, they'll really lose their interest. It looks as if we don't really mean what we say about wanting them to become self-reliant and responsible."

Rose shook her head. "That's really too bad, Kelly," she said. "I wish you had checked with me first. I just don't see what I can do."

24. Is My Face Red?

It was a hot, sticky day, and the boys and their counselor, Mark, were sitting in the shade taking a break. Bruce, a twelve year old well known at camp for his sense of humor, took advantage of the opportunity to tell a joke.

A lady walked into an ice cream shop and ordered a chocolate cone. The clerk said, "We have thirteen wonderful flavors and we rarely run out, but we're out of chocolate today. We have vanilla fudge, chocolate mint, strawberry, butter brickle, and hazelnut, but no chocolate."

"Well, okay," she says. "Let me look at the other flavors." So she looks for a long time, then she says, "There are a lot of choices here, but let's keep it simple. I'll have chocolate."

"I'm sorry," the clerk replied. "I guess I wasn't clear. We're out of chocolate."

"Okay. Let me think about it again." When she was ready, she smiled and said, "I think I've decided on chocolate!"

The clerk looked at her. "Lady, how do you spell 'tutti' as in 'tutti frutti'?"

"T-u-t-t-i."

"How do you spell 'straw' as in 'strawberry'?"

"S-t-r-a-w."

"How do you spell 'frick' as in 'chocolate'?"

The lady paused. "There's no frick-in chocolate!"

"Okay," said Mark, joining in the laughter. "Shall we get back to work?"

"Wait a minute," Lenny responded, "I have a joke, too." Lenny was a little younger than the others, about eleven, but big and mature for his age.

Everyone sat back again to listen as Mark nodded his assent. "It's a fairly long one," Lenny began. "There was this traveling salesman whose car got stuck late at night on a country road near an old farmhouse." Mark, beginning to feel a bit uneasy, shifted his position as Lenny continued. The joke began to deteriorate rapidly through profanity to obscenity, until Mark felt he had to interrupt.

"Lenny, I think we've heard enough of that one," he said. "You know you shouldn't have told that story."

The boy looked a little hurt. "But I heard one of the counselors tell it to some of the others last night. They were telling a lot of jokes and they were so loud they woke me up." The other boys began to snicker as Lenny continued talking. "Don't you want to hear the rest of it?" he asked.

25. A Child with a Difference

The director had told Chris in advance that one of the campers scheduled to be in his cabin, Jared, was a bed wetter. Jared was eleven years old, the same age as the other boys in his group. He had refused to go to an overnight camp before this season, apparently because of his bed-wetting. Chris, an experienced counselor, had never had any real experience with this problem, and he was somewhat apprehensive. He had been glad to have the opportunity to discuss it with the director in advance.

"Children may have a variety of behavioral problems," he was told, "but their adjustment problems are quite similar. It's a matter of emphasizing the child's strengths, what he can contribute, instead of emphasizing his weaknesses." The director had pointed out that there was apparently nothing physically wrong with the boy, and that the actual cause of his bed-wetting was a mystery. Together, they had developed the plan that Chris would follow.

When the campers arrived, Chris made a point to meet and talk with Jared as soon as possible. They discussed camp and the activities generally for a while, and Chris could see that Jared was tense and worried. Jared did not mention the fact that he was a bed wetter until Chris brought it up. "I know you have a problem with bed-wetting, Jared," he said, "and I want you to know that I'll be glad to help in any way I can."

"What I'm worried about," replied Jared, "is how the guys'll treat me. That's why I never went to camp before — only day camp. I was afraid, and I'm still not sure that coming this year was a good idea."

"How often does it happen?" asked Chris.

"Almost every night," was the reply, "even when my parents wake me up to go to the bathroom. I just can't seem to stop it, and I don't know why." There was a short pause, and then Jared added hastily, "But I won't cause any problems. I'll take care of my stuff."

"I'm really not so concerned about that," said Chris, "but I do want you to be happy here. There's no reason why you can't be, either."

"But they'll all laugh at me," said Jared.

"I don't think so," replied Chris. "At least, not if they understand that it's something you can't help. After all, everybody has some kind of problem or weakness; it's just that some are more obvious."

"Do you really think so?" pressed the worried boy.

"Maybe we should discuss it with the group tonight before bedtime," said Chris. "Then it won't come as a surprise."

Jared thought for a few moments, then nodded. "That sounds like a good idea," he said, but Chris could tell that the boy was still worried.

That evening, just before lights out, Chris led a discussion during which they talked about their plans for the camp season ahead. Chris pointed out the skills represented by various members of the group, and he mentioned that everyone had weaknesses as well. He gave a few other examples before telling the boys about Jared's bed-wetting. They had many questions, and Jared joined with Chris in trying to give the answers.

The days that followed passed quickly and smoothly. The boys lived, worked, and played together harmoniously. They all seemed happy and, although Jared wet his bed almost every night, it did not seem to affect his acceptance by the others. He was cheerful and well liked, and he made certain that his special problem caused his counselor and his cabinmates as little trouble as possible. There was often an unpleasant odor in the cabin, especially in the morning and on damp days, but little was said about it. Jared told Chris more than once how much he was enjoying camp and how glad he was that he had finally decided to come.

During the second week of camp, Chris began to sense that tension was building up in the group. He traced most of it to stiff competition between two of the boys. As a result, the group seemed to be splitting into two factions, its unity rapidly disappearing in spite of Chris's efforts to restore the spirit that had existed before. A cold, rainy spell of several days' duration that kept the group indoors most of the time served to aggravate the situation.

The urine odor began to be a problem, not because it was that much worse, but because people were getting tired of it. It was embarrassing Jared, and it was beginning to annoy the other boys, who were forced by the weather to remain in the cabin for so much of the time and to deal with the leadership struggle as well. Chris's experience told him that some kind of reaction was to be expected, so he was not taken completely by surprise one day when he heard loud voices coming from his cabin as he approached.

"Only sissies wet their beds! Why don't you cut out that baby stuff? We tried to be nice about it, but we just can't stand it anymore!"

Angrily, Chris ran into the cabin. He saw Jared sitting on his bed, obviously embarrassed, and practically in tears. "What is this?" Chris shouted. "What's going on here?"

The other campers immediately looked at the floor, and seemed genuinely ashamed of themselves. Finally, one spoke. "We're sorry, Jared," he said. "Honest, we really do like you. It's just that we can't stand it anymore!"

26. Believe It or Not

Brandi returned to the cabin from her archery activity a little earlier than everyone else and used the opportunity to take Tammy's camera from her suitcase. Brandi had been admiring the camera since the first day. It did so many things and looked so nice. As she was thinking about how neat it would be to have such a camera, she was interrupted by the sight of a cabinmate coming down the path.

Reacting quickly, she shoved it under Michelle's sleeping bag, ran to her own bed, and sprawled out in a casual pose. Later that morning, Tammy was walking by Michelle's bed and noticed a familiar camera strap sticking out from under the sleeping bag. Pulling it out and confirming that it was her camera, she called out, "Hey, why is my camera on your bed, Michelle?"

The answer came from across the room. "I don't know, I didn't put it there."

"It was in my suitcase. Someone must have put it on your bed. Are you sure it wasn't you?"

"Yes, of course. I would know if I did it, wouldn't I?"

"But it got out of my suitcase somehow. No one else would take it out and put it under your sleeping bag. That doesn't make any sense. You must have stolen it!"

"I did not, you ass. How could I, with everyone around all the time?"

Tammy stormed out the door to Denise, their counselor, who was on the porch. "Michelle stole my camera out of my suitcase. I caught her and now she's lying. I found it underneath her sleeping bag and it couldn't have gotten there unless she took it. It was in my suitcase this morning and she took it out."

"Whoa, slow down," cautioned Denise. "One thing at a time. How could you see it underneath her sleeping bag. Why were you looking there?"

"I wasn't! The strap was peeking out and I saw it." Tammy's voice began to express her frustration. "She stole it!"

Denise got up, dreading what was coming. "All right, let's look into it."

27. A Rude Awakening

"No, David, I'm sure my kids weren't involved," said Wade to the director. "They wouldn't do a thing like that, and anyway, I'd have known about it if they had." David had told him that some of his fourteen-year-olds were suspected of having broken into the kitchen the night before and stealing a large quantity of food. Several pies were missing, as well as a watermelon, fruit punch, and bags of pretzels and potato chips.

"Maybe you're right," replied David, "but I saw Damian and Jeff, your campers, near the kitchen during the campfire last night."

"You can't make any accusations on the basis of that."

"Take it easy," said David. "Suppose I told you that another one of your boys came to me and told me they did do it?"

Wade was visibly shocked. "There must be some mistake! In the first place, I'm sure my boys wouldn't even think of doing that and, besides, none of them would spread such malicious stories about ... wait a minute! Was it Reggie who told you that?"

David nodded. "He seemed quite upset about it, and he said he came to me because you were on your day off."

"Well, you know Reggie," Wade said. "He'll do almost anything to get attention, and it wouldn't be the first time he told us a lie to make himself look good. The kid's just a misfit, and you can't believe anything simply because he says it."

Reggie was by far the smallest camper in Wade's group and seemingly the most immature. A shy, fearful boy, he had little in common with his cabinmates. Most of them disliked him, and it was true that he tried consistently to seek acceptance from adults rather than from his peers. Indeed, only with adults did he seem to be able to avoid facing downright cruelty.

"Of course Reggie has problems," replied David, "and we know he frequently lies in an effort to gain acceptance. We've been spending a lot of time trying to help him. Now maybe we'll have to do even more. But Wade, not everything that he says need be a lie. Remember, I did see Damian and Jeff near the kitchen. It all seems to add up too well to be a coincidence, doesn't it?"

"Well," said Wade, less antagonistic now, "on the basis of what you've told me, maybe it is worth a little more investigation."

"Look into it, and see what you can find out," David said. "And remember, if it turns out to be true, those kids'll really try to crucify Reggie, even though it may well be that he was right to tell on them."

"I'll check it out, David," said Wade, "but I still think you should look elsewhere."

Wade returned to his cabin. "Where've you been, Wade?" asked Damian. "We were waiting for you."

"Oh, David just told me that some food was stolen from the kitchen last night. He thinks some campers did it, and he wanted to know if I knew anything about it."

"Probably just some hungry kids, or maybe even counselors," said Jeff with a laugh. "I don't know why he calls it stealing. The food's here for us to eat, isn't it?"

"Don't you see the difference?" asked Wade, a little apprehensive. The whole group had gathered around, but no one answered.

"Come on, let's go out and play some ball," Damian finally said.

Wade hesitated a moment, then decided that he would let them go so that he could search the bunk alone. "You guys go," he said. "I have something to do, but I'll be along in a few minutes."

They looked at him, and then they left. After a moment, Wade walked to Damian's bag and opened it. Some of the food was inside. Jeff's suitcase contained more of it, and there was some in two other boys' bags as well. He piled all the food in one spot and wondered what to do.

Just then, Jeff and Damian came back into the cabin. Seeing the food, they stopped. "Reggie," Damian yelled. "That SOB! He didn't want to help, and then he rats on us! I'm going to find him and beat the crap out of him!" He turned and ran out the door.

28. Caught in the Act!

Walking across the cabin area and chatting after lights out one evening, the two counselors responsible for late coverage heard voices and subdued giggling coming from Cabin Nine, which housed a group of twelve- and thirteen-year-olds. Both counselors were experienced enough to recognize that something was suspicious, and they looked at each other only momentarily before nodding and starting toward the sounds. The regular counselor for that cabin was out of camp for a few hours of relaxation.

They stood outside and listened for a few minutes, but the sound showed no sign of subsiding. Quietly, they went up the steps, walked into the cabin, and turned on the overhead light. Naked campers quickly scurried toward their beds and jumped under the covers, but not before the two counselors saw what had been going on. Pornographic pictures and a flashlight lay strewn around the floor where the surprised campers had scattered them in their haste.

29. Just for Fun

Marty hesitated outside the door of the cabin. Inside, his sixteen year olds were in the midst of an excited discussion. They had returned from a campfire with the senior girls about ten minutes earlier, and on the way back Marty had stopped off at the infirmary to ask the nurse about something. He decided not to go into the cabin, lest he inadvertently stop the discussion. Instead, he stood outside and listened.

"You and Joanie were really going at it tonight, Alex," said Denny. "I don't think you got up from that blanket once the whole evening."

"Boy, it was great!" responded Alex. "She sure can kiss. It's too bad she's so stupid, but it didn't matter tonight."

"Don't you think you overdid it, though? You were doing more than kissing! She seems to like you very much, and you're going to be stuck with her, or she'll get hurt."

"If she's willing, why shouldn't I feel her up?" asked Alex in reply. "Do I have to be in love with the girl?"

"As far as I'm concerned, I don't expect to get anything from a girl on the first date," Antonio said. "But after that, she better warm up fast or I'm not going to waste my time and money." Antonio was generally acknowledged to be the leader of the group.

"Yeah, man!" said Brandon. "It's better if you like each other. But if you don't, you might as well have some fun anyway. Besides, with a girl you don't like, you're not afraid of hurting her. Like they say, 'It ain't love, but it ain't bad!'"

Still standing in the shadows outside the cabin, Marty wondered what to do.

30. Sex and the Single Counselor

"Wendy, what are STDs?" someone asked the counselor. Wendy's girls had been paging through and talking about the teen magazines that a few of them had brought to camp. A conversation about the sexual messages in the magazines' advertising, initiated by Wendy, had expanded into numerous other sexual topics.

"STD stands for 'sexually transmitted disease.' Transmitted means something that's given or sent. So an STD is a disease that is transmitted by having sex.

"Like what? AIDS?"

"Yes, AIDS is one of them, and one of the worst. I'm sure you have all heard of AIDS and know something about it, but there are others that you might not know about." Wendy went on to describe several of them.

"They sound nasty. You know a lot about this stuff. Where did you learn it?" one of the girls asked. "Have you ever had one?"

Wendy smiled. "No, I haven't, and I plan to avoid the possibility of ever getting one. You're right, they are nasty."

"Have you ever had sex?" Vanessa had never been overly sensitive or worried about privacy.

Wendy smiled again, but more nervously. "That's really a personal question, and I don't think it would serve any purpose for me to answer it," she said.

The girls snickered and, with knowing looks, started making sarcastic comments. "Sure, Wendy, okay." Wendy turned red and realized that her response would only be interpreted positively.

Vanessa did not let up. "Have you ever masturbated?" she asked.

Wendy wanted to make a foxhole deal with God. "I'll do anything; just get me out of this discussion!" Yet she knew that getting out of it would not help the girls learn. But how should she respond?

31. Just Kidding?

It was late on a warm, sunny afternoon, and the boys were hanging around the campsite waiting for everyone to change their clothes after swimming. It was the next-to-last day of camp, and they were feeling lazy and relaxed. On the way back from the beach, two boys — Mitchell, who was black, and Justin, who was white — had begun a discussion about being sunburned that evolved into other topics about skin color and race. When they reached the campsite, the other members of the group began to get involved.

"Where do different skin colors come from?" said Sean.

"I don't know."

"I think people were just made that way," offered Jonathan.

"Isn't it because of where they're from? Like Africans are black because they live in the hot sun and we're white because we lived in the cold north." At least Sean had a theory.

"What about us Indians? We came from Siberia and we have dark skin," offered Joe.

"You did not come from Siberia. You came from Asia!" The geographical confusion attracted no response.

"If Sean is right, then why don't black people turn white when they move to cold places and white people turn black when they move to warm places?" This from Mitchell, the scientist.

Justin smiled impishly. "I think Africans are black because they came from monkeys!"

Everyone laughed except Mitchell. "Hold on," he responded sharply, an edge beginning to creep into his voice. "White people are white because they're ice people, like polar bears."

"That's better than coming from monkeys!" Justin shot back, as he simulated the knuckle-dragging, chest-beating motions and the sounds of a gorilla. Joe, the Native American, laughed and began to make gorilla sounds.

"Stay out of it, chief!" retorted Mitchell. "At least we walk on our hind legs, unlike polar bears."

"Who are you calling chief?"

"Chief, savage, alkie!"

"Leave him alone!"

"Shut up, nigger!" The other boys were getting into the act.

Devon, the counselor, had been half listening from a distance, but the escalating volume of the last few seconds attracted his attention. He decided he'd better intervene now, if it wasn't too late already.

32. Truth or Consequences

It was late on a weekday night, and the cafe was almost empty. Phil, Rick, Tasha, Kim, and Maggie were enjoying a respite from big bugs and little children. Phil had been talking about his problems with two boys who were very disobedient; in fact, Phil thought that they went out of their way to do the opposite of what he wanted. "I'm not sure what to do. I can't get them under control; they don't listen to me. What do you guys do?"

"Well," said Tasha, "my kids love to swim. If there's a behavior problem, I threaten that we won't go swimming. And if they keep doing it, we don't! The only thing you can do is threaten to take away something they want."

"I do something like that, too," said Rick, "but it's more like a time-out procedure. If someone screws up, they're asked to sit out of the activity for a while. The bigger the problem, the longer they sit. They'll learn that if they want to play the game, they have to play it by our rules."

Phil looked troubled. "But the kids aren't here that long. I hate to deprive them of something they really like to do, because they won't have that many opportunities."

"If they really want to do it they won't screw up."

"That makes their behavior sound so rational, like they're calculating the costs of their actions. I don't think it's that simple," said Maggie.

"Then what do you do, Maggie?"

"We have a demerit system — three strikes and you're out. When someone screws up they get a demerit and, if they get three in one day, then they get a punishment."

"Like what?"

"Like having to clean the bathroom or sweep the volleyball court, or anything they don't like to do. A couple of times we had a kangaroo court and the kids pronounced judgments of what the punishments should be."

Tasha quickly interjected. "But you're using work as a punishment. Don't we want them to do those things voluntarily? We're just teaching them to hate work."

Phil's face showed his frustration. "There must be something that works. I can't go on like this. What do you do, Kim?"

Kim paused and took a deep breath. "The first year I was here I tried those things, but I finally decided that I would never get control of my kids that way. So I quit giving punishments and decided to give rewards instead. I would promise them that if they were good during the day, they would get a treat or something special at night. But a lot of times someone would screw up, and that would create bad feelings about what had been mostly a good day. The hostility would usually be directed at the kids who were least able to handle it. Besides, losing the reward became a kind of punishment. So finally I gave up giving consequences at all, and now I don't have any."

"But that's impossible," Rick said in disbelief. "You can't let the kids walk all over you."

"They don't."

"Then how do you control them?"

"I don't control them. I gave up trying to get control, mostly because I was frustrated. The more control I tried to get, it seemed like the less I had. So I quit trying. It's obvious to me that you have the same problems I do. The difference is that I've admitted that I can't control them, and you haven't. And I think my group gets by as well as most of yours do anyway."

The others looked at each other and back at Kim in skepticism before anyone spoke.

Working within Program Activities and Routines

33. What Price Efficiency?

"Let's get started — we don't have much time." The buzz of voices gradually subsided as Darren, the camp director, called the special staff meeting to order. "Several of you have come to me to discuss the cabin cleanup problem," he began. "There seem to be some problems in this area, and Brett suggested that we talk it over together. I believe you had a suggestion, Brett, didn't you? Maybe we should start from there."

"I think most of us are having the same problem," Brett said. "The kids just don't care about cleanup, and we have to keep pushing them to get it done. Sometimes we even miss part of our first activity because they're so slow. Then they start fights among themselves to find someone to blame. Otherwise, we have to do some of the work for them. The only solution I can see is to give them an incentive, something to work for."

Nate interrupted. "Doesn't the incentive come from the importance of cleanliness for health? We have to interpret it to the kids, but we can't expect them to accept it right away."

"Let's face it, Nate," responded Brett, "kids don't care about cleanliness and never will. We have to give them something they understand. My idea is this: we can set up an inspection system, with numerical ratings for how well the beds are made, how clean the floor is, and so on. Each morning, someone can inspect the cabins. Each week, we'll give a prize to the cabin with the highest average. It doesn't have to be much. Maybe an extra snack. That way, each group will be anxious to outdo the others."

"Wait a minute," Nate said. "That might motivate the kids, but what is it teaching them about cleanup? It seems so artificial. In effect, we'd be saying that having the cleanest cabin is important so that you can have more to eat. There are better reasons to have a clean cabin. Not only that, but why put a premium on having the best? Remember, beyond a certain point neatness and cleanliness can be a fault. Wouldn't we be tending to encourage kids to be compulsive?"

Brett looked at the rest of the counselors and laughed. "That'll be the day! I don't think we'll live to see our kids that clean. But we do have to maintain a certain standard of cleanliness for health reasons, especially since we live so close together at camp. That's necessary whether we use intrinsic motivation or not. Let's be practical. We have to do something about it. We can't go on like this."

Nate shook his head. "Of course we have to keep our cabins reasonably clean and livable. I once went to a camp that used the system you described. It's true that cleanup was sometimes less of a problem there for the first few days, although difficulties similar to ours arose later. But I think we should also consider some of the other things that happened there, apparently as a result of the competitive inspection system. There were times when campers from one cabin snuck into another to mess up the beds and dirty the floors, so they would beat out the other group. Not only does this defeat the purpose of the whole thing, but look at the influence it has on kids' attitudes and behavior. Inspectors were often accused of favoritism, and the bad feeling that developed was reflected in other parts of the program. It seems to me that this kind of thing is inevitable when we create a situation where the motivation is artificial."

"I'm glad you pointed that out, Nate," said Brett. "It'll make us aware of the pitfalls in advance, so we'll be able to avoid them. I don't think any of us would let the kids take it that seriously anyway, do you? We're just using it to get them to do a better job at cleanup. It may also help us teach our kids to work together more effectively in a group, since they'll have a common goal."

"You missed the whole point, Brett," replied Nate with some heat. "Can't you see that counselors tend to get involved too, once you establish a situation like this? They begin to feel that their own effectiveness is on trial, so they drive the kids. I've even seen counselors incite their kids to cheat, or participate in cheating themselves. But this is just an example of what I'm getting at. In and of itself, this kind of system tends to foster exclusiveness and intergroup rivalry, a kind of 'cabin nationalism.' What we have then is a situation where competition among groups is being established in an effort to overcome dissension and disunity within groups. That sounds very much like war logic to me, and I suspect that on a symbolic level, that's what we'd be teaching our kids. It seems to me we'd be wiser to try to solve the problems and conflicts within our groups more directly, where they appear. Don't you see what I mean?"

It was Brett who shook his head this time. "You're always bringing in extraneous reasons to criticize new program ideas. Now you're trying to tell us that this situation can be equated with *war*. That's nonsense! These are just kids, and we're trying to give them some incentive to clean up their cabins. Basically, the kids don't care if the cabins are clean or not. We have to give them a reason to care, or they'll never clean up. We could do it for them, and probably faster, but is that what we're here for? Another way would be to use threats and punishment, but I don't think any of us wants that. So what else can we do? If you're so smart, Nate, what would you suggest?"

Darren spoke for the first time since he had opened the meeting. "Just a minute. You two have been monopolizing the discussion. We'll get to Nate's suggestions in a minute, but first I'd like to hear what some of the rest of us think."

34. After Dark

PPPHHT! Another rude noise led to another round of uncontrollable giggling and snorting in Anthony's cabin of ten year olds. Anthony sighed and buried himself in his sleeping bag. He had tried hard to enforce the campwide lights out and quiet time, but this was the first day of camp for this session and the boys were out of control. For the last two hours he had tried everything — politely asking for quiet, yelling at them, sneaking around in the dark to catch and punish the culprits, and ignoring them — but nothing seemed to work. The more he tried, the worse their behavior became.

He had the same problem with his last group. As the session went on, the boys started going to sleep on their own because they were so tired, but the first night was really tough. He had hoped for better with this group, but it was the same old thing.

I'm not cut out for this, he thought. I should have found a different job this summer. The thought of sleeping in peace and quiet with no responsibility for anyone else sounded so good that he was tempted to pack up and leave right then.

While he was considering his options, he heard a loud crash and a cry of pain. Little rugrats, he thought. What did they do now? He climbed out of bed and turned on the light.

35. When Standards Conflict

"Our parents sent us here to have fun and do what we want," said Anne, defiantly, "and if we want to sit inside and read fashion magazines, that's our business." Ruby looked around the cabin at her fourteen year olds, most of whom were, indeed, stretched out on their beds reading fashion magazines. One was studying her face in the mirror, and two others were talking privately. All had their hair set with rollers or wrapped in towels. Except for mealtimes, they had spent the entire day in the cabin, getting ready for that evening's dance with the boys.

The director, Lisa, had spoken with Ruby more than once about getting the girls involved in camp activities at least some of the time, and Ruby agreed that this was important. Where do I start? she wondered, as she surveyed the scene of ten teenagers who acted as if they couldn't care less. She liked her girls and they seemed to like her, but each time she tried to stimulate their interest in other areas, her efforts were rewarded with fresh retorts or, worse, bored and defiant silence.

Through the window, she noticed that Lisa was coming up the hill toward the cabin, and she stepped outside to meet her. "Lisa, can you spare a few minutes?" she asked. Lisa nodded, noticing that Ruby was upset, and they sat down under a tree. "I feel almost ready to give up," was Ruby's first comment. "These girls are so sophisticated and blasé, but they don't know how much they're missing. If they'd only let themselves, they could enjoy camp activities so much and benefit in other ways, too, but I can't seem to motivate them at all. It's so frustrating. I know they're supposed to be boy-crazy at this age, but I think they need other kinds of experiences at the same time. Some of their behavior isn't even in good taste. I just don't know what to do."

"I think there's no question that what you've said about the girls is true," said Lisa, "and I know how frustrating it can be."

"Sometimes I think we should just take away the magazines and the makeup and force the girls to live in the woods for a few days," replied Ruby. "Maybe something would penetrate then — a sort of shock treatment!"

"That's one possibility. Would you like to try it?"

"I really don't think it would work, Lisa, although it might make me feel a little better, at least for a while. It would cause too much resentment. I guess we couldn't justify the sudden change, either. The kids would think we were being arbitrary and unreasonable."

"Anyway, it's an option for us to consider," said Lisa. "Can you think of any others?"

"Well," replied Ruby, "we can continue to ignore it. They feel that since they — or their parents — paid for camp, they should be allowed to do whatever they please. That's sure different from my idea of what camp should be. We could try to discuss the whole subject of camp and their interests with them, but they seem to know what's coming and get resentful and clam up whenever I start to talk about it."

"You have a good, close relationship with your group, Ruby," said Lisa. "Your girls like you very much. You may be in a position to influence them more than you realize. Be sure to consider that as you weigh the alternatives. And don't be too worried about jeopardizing your relationship with the girls by making your opinions clear. Any relationship that can't survive a little honesty isn't worth much anyway."

"That helps, Lisa," said Ruby. "Thanks a lot. I'll give it another try."

Lisa left, but Ruby remained to think about what they had said. Just as she decided what she would try first, she heard her campers coming out of the cabin.

"Where are you going?" she asked.

As usual, Anne was their spokesperson. "Oh, we're scheduled for the climbing tower this afternoon, but it's too hot," she said casually. "We're going down to the waterfront to dangle our feet in the water and read." They all paused, waiting for Ruby's reply.

36. In the Face of Adversity

Ever since camp had opened, Lynne had been trying to interest her fifteen-year-old campers in cookouts, overnight hikes, and other outdoor activities. To her, these were the essence of camping, the times when campers could get to know each other—and themselves—more intimately than during any other kind of program. But the girls had objected strenuously ever since she first mentioned the idea. They had finally agreed to cook dinner out one evening, almost as a concession to Lynne, but they refused even to discuss a campout.

Lynne felt that they were a little bit afraid, too. Still, she persisted in talking about how much fun she had had on overnights as a camper and told of an especially beautiful spot she knew about not far from camp. Finally, they agreed to visit the site.

Lynne could tell when they started out the next morning that the odds were against her. The girls had all decided against the program already, and they were going primarily to mollify Lynne and to have their opinions confirmed. Finally, she broke into their conversation.

"Girls," she said, "you're talking as if your minds are already made up. I think you owe it to yourselves to go with open minds." Reluctantly, the girls agreed.

Before long, they reached the beginning of the trail to the campsite. As soon as they started to walk through the forest, Lynne could sense that the girls were impressed. The trail led them under tall, majestic evergreens. It was cool and shady, and the air was redolent with the odor of the pines. Fallen needles formed a soft, springy bed on which they walked, and the trail markers were the only visible evidence that anyone had ever been there before. Suddenly, they came to a clearing and, beyond, a crystal-clear lake shimmering in the sunlight. "This," said Lynne softly, "is the spot I had in mind."

The girls stood in silence for many seconds, awed by what they saw. "It's a very pretty place," Stacey finally said. Stacey had been the most negative of all the girls at first, so Lynne was especially happy to hear that she liked it. "But what about water?" Stacey continued. "And do we have to dig latrines?"

"Aren't there any toilets?" asked Sabrina, looking a little alarmed.

"All we'll need is drinking water," said Lynne, "and we can bring that in our canteens. We'll have an extra supply in the truck parked out at the road, and that's not so far. Our water for washing can come right from the lake. There is a pit toilet down that trail."

"You're kidding," said Sabrina. "That sounds horrible! I wouldn't like that at all!"

"Come on, Sabrina, it wouldn't be all that bad," said Jackie, one of only a few who had been on camping trips before. "But what would we do here, Lynne?" she asked.

"We'll only be here for about a day," answered Lynne, "and there's plenty for us to do. Part of the time we'll be fixing up our campsite and making meals. Then we can swim in the lake and hike up to a fire tower near here. You can see the whole countryside from the top. There's natural clay around to make things with, and we can use the fire to bake them. We can always play games, and it's a nice place just to sit and think, write, draw, or whatever you feel like. Isn't it quiet and relaxing?"

On the way back, the girls discussed the campout proposal at length. It was clear that they were considering it seriously. In spite of marked reluctance and opposition on the part of some, the group decided to go. There was no great enthusiasm, but Lynne was pleased that they were willing to try. Enthusiasm would come later, if they had a good experience this time.

After a couple days of planning, they departed on schedule. They worked well together, and before long the tents were up and a comfortable and attractive campsite had been created. Dinner was prepared and eaten with a minimum of confusion and a maximum of enjoyment, and the girls' spirits seemed to be improving by the minute. After dinner, they gathered around the fire for songs and stories. The campfire ended with roasted marshmallows, then all retired to their tents. Lynne was very tired, but she waited until the girls' chatter had died down before she let herself drift off to sleep.

Suddenly she awoke to the sound of thunder. There was no rain yet, and none of the girls seemed to be awake, so she stayed where she was. It was a little after one o'clock; she had slept for about two hours.

The thunder grew louder and, within a few minutes, the rain began to fall. Lynne dozed to the pleasant sound of rain falling on the rain fly, but she soon began to hear some of the girls calling her. "Lynne, I'm getting wet. What should I do?" It became evident that the storm was more than a passing shower and that some of the tents were not well protected.

Lynne had covered their wood, and it was still dry. With Jackie's help, she managed to rig up a cover over the fireplace, and they got a fire started. Damp and cold, most of the girls came out of their tents and stood disconsolately around the fire, under the protecting edges of the canvas. The rain gradually subsided. When Lynne began to see some stars through the clouds, she knew that the weather was clearing, but she was afraid that it was too late. "Let's get changed into dry clothes and back into bed!" she said with all the enthusiasm she could muster.

"Are you kidding?" the girls said. "We're going to get sick. Let's go back to camp."

"We didn't want to come here in the first place," moaned Sabrina. "Now we're all soaked and cold."

The other girls echoed her complaints. "We made the decision to come," said Sabrina, "so now we're deciding to go home. Anyway, we told you it was a lousy idea. Let's get out of here." She turned to the other girls. "Come on, let's go." Several of the girls made a move to follow her, then paused and looked inquiringly at Lynne.

Lynne thought quickly. If they leave under these circumstances, they'll probably never try it again. Besides, can I let them experience a defeat when they haven't even put up a fight? They could beat this and have fun so easily — and something to talk about back home — if they'd only try, but they don't know how strong they really are. Yet, they're so demoralized. If I try to force them to stay....

37. An Ambitious Project

"Don't you think it would be fun for us to build something to be a permanent addition to camp?" asked Alan. His group of nine year olds, seated around him on the floor of the cabin, paused for a moment to think about the suggestion.

"Some of us who were here last year built that fireplace near the lake, the one we used for our hot dog roast," said Justin. "That was lots of fun. Let's make another one." The others agreed and wanted to get started immediately, but Alan was not so sure.

"That was a good project," he said, "and it's used by just about every group in camp. Do we really need another one, though? There are several around camp already. Besides, maybe you're ready to tackle something a little more difficult. You're a year older now, you know."

"Well, what else could we do, Alan?" asked Timmy.

"Let's see what else we can think of," responded Alan. "Do you have any ideas?" They certainly did, and almost every boy in the group shouted at least one suggestion. None seemed to gain much support, however, and after a few minutes the noise subsided.

Timmy broke the silence. "Could we build a houseboat?" he asked. The others looked interested.

"That's an idea," said Alan. "What would we do with it?"

"Well," Timmy answered, "kids could use it to play in, like we play in the treehouse that the seniors built last year. Only this could be on the lake instead of up in a tree."

The group's enthusiasm was obvious and unrestrained. "Let's talk about it a little before we decide," said Alan. "We'd better plan this pretty carefully." Alan was getting excited about it, too.

They spent parts of the next two days discussing their project and drafting ambitious plans on paper. Alan had to be alert to scale down their proposals, or the finished product would be larger than the lake itself. Finally, they had developed a plan that pleased them and seemed to Alan to be within the realm of practicability. The cabin was to be no larger than the tree house, about six feet by eight feet, on top of a barge-like floor.

"Do you really think they'll let us do it?" asked Anthony.

"Sure, why not?" Alan replied. "It's a good idea, and we've planned it carefully."

Next, they made a list of the supplies and tools they would need. Alan began to feel some misgivings when he realized what would be required, and he decided that he had better discuss the project with the director or the caretaker before it went any further. He had difficulty persuading his enthusiastic campers of this, however. They wanted to start building, and it was only after Alan explained that some of the supplies would have to be ordered that they agreed to a delay.

Alan walked over to see Bill, the camp caretaker, and told him of the boys' plans. Bill looked at the drawings, shaking his head. "Those kids aren't going to be able to do this," he said. He proceeded to explain some of the structural complexities that they had not anticipated. "I'm not even sure you have the skill for it, Alan," he concluded.

Alan realized that Bill was right. "There's a lot I didn't think of, Bill," he said. "I can see that now. But the kids' hearts are so set on it. Maybe we should let them try anyway; maybe they'll learn something."

"I guess that's up to you," Bill said. "But I don't know what good it does to let kids try something you know will end in failure. It'll probably never be finished, and all the stuff'll be wasted. That's nothing to teach kids — they're too darn wasteful already. Or else you'll end up finishing it yourself, and that's no good either. Let them do something they can really do. There's lots of rocks around and I'll give you some cement. They can build another fireplace."

"Thanks, Bill," replied Alan dejectedly, "I'll have to think about it first. I'll let you know."

As he walked back to the cabin, Alan hoped the group's enthusiasm had worn off. He had scarcely started, however, when he saw his campers running toward him. The first two jumped into his arms, shouting, and the others were close behind.

"Let's go, Alan."

"We know the perfect place to build it, so it'll be easy to launch."

"All right, Alan!"

"When do we start?"

38. Their True Colors?

"Let's go, guys!" Jen exclaimed. "We've got our volleyball game against the blues in five minutes. Remember, we lose points if we're late."

"All right, let's go, seniors! We're gonna kill 'em and win the whole thing!" yelled Margie, the red team's captain, as the rest of the team headed toward the door.

"Have fun, guys," said Jen, sensing that maybe they were a little too "high." "Remember, winning is great, but fun and sportsmanship are what it's all about."

"Yeah, yeah, we know," someone responded as they left.

"I'll be cheering you on," Jen called after them. "I have to drop something at the office, and then I'll be there.

A few minutes later, Jen heard a commotion coming from the volleyball court as she approached. The blue team had not arrived yet, but she could see that her team members were up in arms, yelling at Ally. "You guys take this whole thing too seriously," she heard Ally respond. "I don't want to play anymore!"

"Good! We didn't want you anyway — you just keep messing up!" responded Margie.

"Whoa," shouted Jen as she covered the last few steps to the court. "What happened to sportsmanship? I'm disappointed in you guys. You know the rules about that. We'll just have to forfeit the game."

That evening, when the staff met for its daily check-in on the day's events, Jen explained why her team had forfeited in volleyball and added that she was distressed at the way the kids were reacting to the competition.

Jeff disagreed. "Maybe you're getting a little carried away. It was one incident! You didn't have to cancel the game; the kids were really upset. Maybe you could have just pulled certain kids out instead."

"I don't think you understand my point, Jeff" answered Jen. "If this kind of incident can occur, then maybe they're not understanding what competition is meant to teach — sportsmanship, cooperation, things like that. I think the competitive aspect has taken over. Maybe we should just cancel the whole thing."

39. Bogged Down?

The girls were excited about their first real rock-climbing trip. They would be leaving in the morning, and they were busy getting their gear ready, figuring out what they wanted to bring for lunch and snacks, and practicing climbing holds on their bunk beds and cabin walls.

Bonnie, their counselor, had some rope and a few harnesses and began to show them some knots and how the belaying system worked. "The end of the rope goes through your harness like this," she explained, "and then it follows back through the figure eight. Watch, and then you can each try it."

As she was demonstrating, Scott from the nature center knocked on the cabin door. "Hey, Bonnie, are you guys coming down to the center? You're scheduled for a bog walk at four, and it's after that already. You arranged for it last week."

"Scott, I'm sorry," she replied. "We were so busy that I just forgot. We're going on a rock-climbing trip in the morning. Let's get ready to go, girls," she continued, turning to the group. "Let's hurry so we don't miss it. You can leave everything where it is 'til we get back."

"That's okay. I'll see you down there in a few minutes," said Scott, turning to leave.

As some of the girls started half-heartedly to put on their shoes, Amanda spoke up. "Do we have to go, Bonnie? We're all excited about getting ready for tomorrow, and we don't want to go for a bog walk right now. Let's stay here instead." The other girls called out and nodded their agreement, and everyone looked at Bonnie for her answer.

40. Tradition!

"But why should we have to go to a flag ceremony if we don't want to?" protested Crissy. "That's not why we came."

"We have a tradition here at camp," replied Evie, her counselor, to the group of fourteen and fifteen year olds, "that each morning the whole camp gathers around the flagpole for the pledge of allegiance and an inspirational message from the camp director. That way, we begin the day thinking about our commitments and values. It's a way for us to make a public statement about who we are and what we believe, and to do it as a group. Every group is expected to do it. It's part of the tradition of being a member of this camp community."

"That sounds good," responded Maggie, "but it should be voluntary. How can you make people do it? It feels like a forced commitment, and some of us aren't so hot on this patriotism stuff either. Besides, the director's inspiration is not always so inspirational!"

"How can you say that I have to work to maintain someone else's tradition?" added Sue. "I've never been here before and I may never be here again, so what does it have to do with me? I'd feel like some kind of hypocrite if I did it even though deep down I knew I didn't want to."

"That's not the point," said Evie. "You're part of this community for now, so why not respect its traditions and those of us who do feel that it's important? This is one of the ways we build a feeling of community, and that makes the summer better for all of us."

"But that *is* the point!" Crissy was speaking again. "Why would it be disrespectful to others for us not to participate? Suppose we stayed in our cabin, out of sight of the others. I agree that it wouldn't be right for us to do anything that would interfere with what other people want to do, but as long as we choose to stay away, what's the problem?"

It seemed to Evie that they had been going around the same

circle for the last hour, and she wished that she could offer more satisfying answers. She felt inadequately prepared and wished that she could discuss the problem with someone more experienced. But she was also concerned that stopping the discussion now would tend to reinforce the girls' point of view. "It's partly a matter of the added spirit that comes from doing things together," she finally said. "The effort draws us closer to each other, and camp becomes a better, richer place for all of us. We're each responsible to everyone else in camp for the general welfare, and this is part of it."

"But what good is that if someone doesn't feel it?" asked Maggie. "Doing something I don't want to do would just make me angry and frustrated, and that certainly wouldn't help camp spirit — or mine, either. We can understand why *you* have to participate — to set a good example. But why do we?"

41. Beyond Belief?

"Okay, guys, time to get ready for services," said Alan to his group of fourteen year olds. "I have to check something at the office, but I'll be back in a few minutes. Be sure to be ready so we can get to the chapel on time."

When he got back, the group appeared to be ready to go, but Alan noticed that Darryl was missing. "Hey, you guys look great!" he said. "But where's Darryl?"

"He went down to the waterfront."

"Is he okay?" No one seemed to know, so Alan told them to go ahead, and he would meet them there.

As he approached the waterfront, Alan was surprised to see Darryl sitting on the grass, apparently relaxing, and not dressed for services. "Hey, Darryl, I was looking for you," he called. "Is everything all right?"

"Sure. Why wouldn't it be?"

"Well, everyone else just went to services. You're not even dressed yet," replied Alan.

After a brief pause, Darryl answered. "I'm not going."

"Why not?"

"I don't believe in this religion stuff. I don't even believe in God, so why should I go to services?"

"Do you want to talk about it?"

"No."

"Well, if you want to do that sometime, I'll be around, so let me know. That's part of the reason I'm here. For now, let's go to services."

"There's no reason for me to go."

"Darryl," responded Alan, "I'm not here to tell you what to believe in, but religious services are an important part of the program here, and I think it's appropriate for everyone to show up. Besides, people have found worth in worship for generations. The two words even come from the same root, worth and worship. Maybe you should at least be exposed to it." Alan suddenly stopped, wondering whether he was beginning to sound too preachy.

"No, thanks," Darryl responded. "I just don't want to."

Alan paused for a moment before deciding how to respond. "Okay, you can stay here this time, but I want you to think about it, and I hope I'll see you there next week." Darryl shrugged, and Alan walked back toward the chapel.

All week, Alan sensed that Darryl was avoiding him, and the boy was nowhere to be found when it was time for services. Alan again sent the rest of the group ahead and went to the waterfront, where he found the boy lying down, twirling a blade of grass between his teeth. "Hey, I thought we agreed that you would go to services this week!"

"*You* said that, but I really don't want to. I don't believe in it, so there's no point," responded Darryl.

"That puzzles me," responded Alan. "You've been here before, and you know that attending services is one of the camp's expectations. Why did you come back if that was a problem for you?"

"I don't know. I guess I didn't really think that much about it last year, so it didn't occur to me."

"Darryl," Alan continued, "my offer to talk about it still stands, but you and every other member of this community are expected — really, required — to attend services. You don't have to pray, but maybe you can use the time productively by sitting quietly and thinking about some of the issues involved — belief in God, ethical behavior, and so on."

"Where has all this stuff gotten us?" Darryl countered, disgustedly. "There seems to be at least as much suffering and injustice in the world as there ever was! But that's not the point. What I want to know is why we have to attend services if we would really rather not."

Alan was beginning to get a little impatient. "We can talk about that later," he said. "But I want you to come with me to the chapel in the meantime."

"Fine, if that'll make you happy!" responded Darryl arrogantly.

I wonder if I handled that well, Alan thought uncertainly as he walked toward the chapel. His question was answered when, shortly after the service started, Darryl had to be removed due to his disruptiveness. Even the others in the group seemed to be annoyed with him.

When Alan approached Darryl later to talk about the incident, the boy did not wait for him to begin. "I warned you!" Darryl snorted, apparently more in frustration than in anger. "There's no point in my being there, and you shouldn't try to make someone do something he doesn't believe in!"

Working Professionally

42. The Role of a Leader

"Yes, I knew they were going on the raid," said Nick. "But I promised that I wouldn't stop them. They didn't do any real damage, anyway."

"That's not the point, Nick," persisted Graham, the director. "The important point is, you accepted something that both you and they knew was completely against our regulations. What you did was a form of collusion with your campers. By siding with them and against authority, you really forfeited your position as a counselor. In effect, you let yourself act like a camper again. That's always a temptation, but a good leader has to be able to resist."

Nick was sincerely confused. After many years as an outstanding camper, he had finally attained the counselor status that he had coveted for so long. He had a close relationship with his thirteen-year-old campers, and he had thought he was doing a good job.

"But how can I be a good counselor if my boys don't trust me and like me?" he asked. "If they didn't trust me, then they wouldn't tell me things like this at all. How can I betray their trust? Besides, you have to expect boys to break the rules once in a while."

"Of course I expect *children* to break the rules from time to time," said Graham, emphasizing "children." "What I'm saying is that, if we adults don't correct them when they do, they'll never learn to be mature, responsible people. We expect this kind of behavior, and we can understand it, but we certainly shouldn't accept it. You know, it's important for children to learn that authority is not a dirty word. Reasonable rules are necessary if people are going to be able to live together comfortably, and only immature people find them oppressive.

"As for being popular with your campers," he continued, "don't overemphasize it. Remember that kids may gripe and complain, but they really want someone to set limits for them, someone who'll put on the brakes. Their inner controls aren't strong enough yet. They need reassurance that the adults around agree on the limits and won't let them go too far and maybe hurt themselves. Otherwise, they get confused and anxious, and their behavior becomes more and more extreme as they try to find the limits. Limits give them security, but they can't get that if you become virtually one of them. Remember, a father shouldn't be a pal to his son — a son can find lots of pals. The father should be a father to him. You're in the same position. You should always accept the boy, but not necessarily all of his behavior."

"But they just want to have a good time," Nick replied. "They don't want to feel that someone's always watching them. I'd be a louse if I called them on all the things they do that aren't according to the book. Everyone likes to break the rules now and then, just to feel he's getting away with something."

"You'll have to make up your mind," said Graham, looking at Nick intently. "Do you want to be a camper or a counselor? A child or an adult?"

Deep in thought, Nick walked back toward his cabin. The boys were sitting around on their beds talking in muffled tones, but were obviously excited about something. "Keep this quiet, Nick," said one of the boys. "We're meeting the girls out at the campsite around midnight. No groups are scheduled to be out there tonight, are there?"

43. Do It or Else!

Paul had told the boys three times not to throw stones, and he was beginning to get annoyed. They had arrived at the waterfront a little early, and the gravel had proved to be too much of a temptation for some of them as they waited for the lifeguard to unlock the rowboats and canoes. Whenever Paul looked away, stones somehow seemed to fly over the boats and toward the water. Unfortunately, some of them didn't quite make it over the boats and bounced off the hulls with loud bangs.

Finally, Paul lost control. "I'm going to drown the next person to throw a stone!" he yelled. That ought to stop it, he thought.

Less than a minute later, he turned just in time to see Justin slinging a rock as far as he could. Insulted that the boy did not take him seriously, Paul marched over to Justin, grabbed him by the arm, and dragged him into the water. Justin began screaming and struggling, but Paul pulled harder.

As he was about to dunk the boy, he felt a hand firmly grab his arm. "That's enough, Paul. Stop it!" Jack, his co-counselor, who had just arrived, was pulling him back.

Paul paused, but he was tempted to continue anyway. His fury was making it difficult to think. Reluctantly, he released his hold on Justin, who scrambled to safety. Paul looked around, shrugged his shoulders, and slowly waded back to shore, where Jack and the boys were watching to see what he would do next. As the depth of the water decreased, his embarrassment increased.

44. Let's Talk

Although she was in her first year as a counselor, Melissa had developed an excellent rapport with the campers, even beyond those in her own group. Everyone noticed how she was always there for kids to talk to. One day, on the way to the drama group she led, she heard a voice from behind her:

"Melissa, Melissa, wait up a second!"

"Hi, Jimmy, what's up?" she responded. "How about joining one of the drama groups?"

"Maybe, but I really need to talk to you about something."

"Sure, you know I'm always here for you, but can it wait until after my next group? It starts now."

"I know, I know, but I have to talk to you! Please?"

Melissa glanced down at her watch. "I'll tell you what, we'll talk for a few minutes, but then I'll have to go because the group will be waiting, okay?"

"Great!" Jimmy exclaimed.

Later that afternoon, John, the counselor of the group that had been waiting for Melissa, approached her. "What happened to you this morning? Our group was waiting for half an hour!"

"I'm really sorry. Jimmy needed to talk, and he said it couldn't wait."

"I'm sure that's true, but this isn't the first time that this has happened," countered John. "I also heard that Jimmy's counselor was looking for him because they were supposed to go to the lake, and he'll do anything to get out of swimming. By the way, I was in their bunk later on and I overheard the kids saying how whenever they want to get out of something, they go talk to 'her.' I don't know if they were referring to you, but...are you sure he needed to speak to you right then?"

Melissa frowned. "I wondered what the big deal was," she responded. "He really didn't seem to have that much to say. I'll have to give that a little more thought."

The next morning, on the way to soccer, Donnie, a boy from Jimmy's bunk approached her. "Melissa, do you have a minute? I really need to talk. My counselor hates me!"

45. A Touching Story

"So you see, Mr. Tom," Brian continued tearfully, "I really shouldn't be here. I should be home, helping my mother."

Tom had initiated the conversation in an effort to learn why, although Brian participated in all the activities and was one of the most popular campers in the group, he never seemed to be really happy. Little had Tom expected to hear that Brian's father had left their home shortly before camp started, leaving the twelve year old's mother with his two preschool siblings and no income except what she earned in a sales job and part-time work driving a taxi at night. The boy had taken care of the little ones after school before camp started, but since then his mother had had to juggle things to make ends meet. They had recently come to the city from another area, so they had few local connections. That explains things, thought Tom. He feels guilty that he is here and can't allow himself to really enjoy it.

Later that day, Tom was discussing the situation with several of the other counselors, trying to decide what to do. "I really wanted to put my arm around him and and tell him that having fun at camp would be what his mother wanted most for him, and it would strengthen him to be even more helpful to her when he went home. But it seemed so cold just to say that without..."

"I know," interrupted Cary. "How can you do something like that without putting your arm around him or somehow showing him physically that you understand; yet they tell us to be very careful about that!"

"Exactly!" responded Tom. "I felt paralyzed, and I'm afraid I didn't handle the situation very well as a result. Why don't they trust us to do the right thing?"

"It's a tough one," said Hank, the oldest and most experienced counselor in the group. "There have been many lawsuits on this issue by now where questions of physical or sexual abuse have been raised. A camp can be wiped out in such a case, even if it wins, because people are never sure that the allegations were wrong and may avoid that camp. There are certainly enough others to choose from these days. So everyone is running scared, and they don't want to take any chances."

"But then how can we do our jobs?" asked Cary, obviously discouraged.

"It's a real problem," acknowledged Hank. "There are also insurance issues involved. Things have changed, but the law of self-preservation has not been repealed. Maybe we have to learn to live with it. I don't find it easy, either. It seems like almost everything is in the gray area these days."

On his way back to the cabin, Tom saw Brian running toward him. Sobbing, the boy threw himself into Tom's arms. "My mom just called," he cried. "My brother and sister are sick and she had to stay home to take care of them. I think she's going to lose her job!"

46. What Can I Say?

The boys were complaining during their swim time. "Careful now, we don't want to have too much fun and get yelled at by the lifeguard!"

"We can't splash, we can't have chicken fights, we can't throw each other up in the air, we can't dunk each other...."

"Can't, can't, can't, can't, can't. There isn't anything we *can* do."

As the swim period progressed, fewer and fewer campers were in the water, even though it was very hot. They were losing interest in swimming and, after a while, Brad's boys asked him if they could leave. Walking slowly back to the cabin behind his campers, Brad could tell that they were still seething at Tom, the lifeguard. He was hardly prepared, however, for the hostility that greeted him when they got back.

"What does he think we are — babies?" shouted Alfredo. "Everybody's always worried about us getting hurt, but no one wants us to have any fun. Tom's an ass. Can't you talk to him, Brad? We came here to have fun, not to follow stupid rules!"

A little annoyed now, Brad responded firmly. "Now wait a minute, all of you! Either we're going to calm down and discuss this sensibly or we won't discuss it at all." The boys were usually reasonable and cooperative, thought Brad. Never had he seen them so angry.

When Alfredo spoke again, it was in a somewhat softer tone, but he was obviously still disturbed. "Brad, can we have a cabin meeting to discuss this? Now?" The others agreed with Alfredo's request, but Brad suggested that they first take a few minutes to change out of their wet swim suits. He hoped this break would help them cool off emotionally. Brad felt as the campers did that the new rules were overcautious and unreasonable, although he had been careful not to let them know of his opposition. In fact, Brad had tried to express his own reservations after Tom had told the staff of the new rules, but Tom had refused to discuss the matter at all.

Brad wondered how he could best respond to his campers without violating his responsibility to support camp policy. He felt that it would be hard for him to defend the reasonableness of the new restrictions and at the same time maintain his reputation for fairness and honesty with the boys.

When they had finished changing, the campers sat on the porch of the cabin, as they usually did when there was a matter of general concern to be discussed. As they gathered, they resumed their complaining, and it was evident that the short respite had done little if anything to reduce the tension. Brad thought it best to let the boys express their resentment freely at first, so he said little and listened. Many incidents of supposed "babying" were cited, but the hostility seemed focused on "Tom's waterfront rules."

Suddenly, the group seemed to realize that Brad had said very little and had not committed himself at all. "What do you think about all this, Brad?" asked Alfredo. "You haven't told us your opinion. Tom really is an ass, isn't he?"

47. Going to Pot

"But you can't kick her out of camp, Vlc. She needs to be here," Laura pleaded. Laura had caught Sonia smoking marijuana — a clear violation of camp rules as well as state law. She had confiscated the marijuana and reported the incident to Vic, the program director. Now she wished she had not reported it, because Sonia, while a little crude, had begun to respond to Laura's attention and the healthy camp atmosphere and was slowly losing her tough-girl facade.

"I agree that she needs to be here," said Vic, "but this is something we can't ignore. She broke the law and I could report her to the authorities, but instead I'll just send her home. She's lucky she's not in more trouble."

"So you're going to send her home, where she can get all the pot she wants and where she apparently doesn't get much love? That doesn't make sense, Vic. How can you justify it? She's been acting almost like a normal girl her age the last few days. And yesterday she volunteered to clean the cabin for everyone else, something I don't expect from any of my girls. Don't tell me that one joint cancels all the good that's happened to her here!"

"I'm not claiming that this is a good outcome, but we can't ignore what she did, either. She knew the rules. We have to set a good example for the other campers, too. And how can we risk being seen by the public as tolerating lawbreaking behavior? I also have a responsibility to our sponsors, who would be upset if this weren't handled properly. This is one of the rules that can't be bent. Sonia stepped on the wrong side, and I have no choice. I'm sorry, but she's going to have to leave."

"Then I'm not sure I can work here anymore, Vic," responded Laura. "Girls like Sonia are the reason I came to camp." She slammed the door a little too hard on the way out, her eyes brimming with tears. How can I possibly tell Sonia? she thought. There must be something I can do about this.

48. Local Yokels

On their night off, Jenny and Claire drove to town to eat out. While they were at the restaurant, they began talking with Jim and Scott, two local residents who were eating dinner after work. After a friendly conversation, the two young men asked the girls if they could come out to camp to see them. Jenny and Claire thought that would be nice and invited them to visit on Wednesday, when there was to be a campwide water carnival. Not only did they visit on Wednesday, but they also came on Thursday and Friday. While at camp, they spent most of their time finding opportunities to talk to their new friends.

After the third visit, Claire asked Jenny, "Aren't you getting a little tired of them coming here all the time? They're nice, but it's getting hard for me to do my job with them hanging around and showing off."

"Me, too," responded Jenny. "Scott hasn't shown much interest in the kids and makes it more difficult for us to pay attention to what we should be doing."

"Let's ask them to hang out somewhere else," suggested Claire, and Jenny agreed.

The next day they talked with Jim and Scott and explained the problem. The visitors did not appear to understand but agreed to give them more space. They came to camp the next few nights, but they spent most of their time with other staff members.

A few days later, Jennie and Claire were sitting in the staff lounge with several other counselors. "I was trying to get one of my kids into the water for the first time," Sean was saying to them, "and that friend of yours — Jim — was there splashing kids. He splashed my kid unexpectedly, and now the kid won't go anywhere near the water. Can you do something about getting him out of here?"

"Yeah," Denise added, "they're always around, like this is their playground or something."

Jenny and Claire looked at each other, each hoping that the other would say something first.

49. Out of Bounds

It was Saturday night, and some of the staff members were gathered at a park on the opposite end of the lake from the camp to have a few beers and relax. Most of the group were above the legal drinking age, but Steve, Nathan, and Amy were not. "They told us drinking was against the rules," Mylo was saying, "but I assumed that meant on camp property or during work time."

"You know, I don't think Tom was clear about that," said Cindy thoughtfully. "He said that drinking was prohibited and that, as the director, he would have to fire anyone he caught drinking, but I don't think that he said anything about what we do on our time off."

"That's not his business anyway," responded Todd from the other side of the campfire. "As long as I don't show up for work drunk or hung over and do my job, what I do in my private life is up to me! They don't *own* me."

"But what about people who are under age?" asked Cindy. "That's breaking a state law, not just a camp rule. If we get caught, can't he fire all of us?"

"It's still our own time," Steve objected. "They can't claim we aren't capable of doing our jobs. It's our day off. We're on duty almost twenty-four hours a day for days in a row, and we deserve to have some time to ourselves. Anyway, it's not like this is the first beer we've ever had, and we're just having a couple. You're not going to get drunk on three beers."

"Yeah, it's not Tom's job to enforce state laws," agreed Todd.

Mylo reached across Nathan and into the cooler for more beers to pass around to the others. "Yours is still in there," he said to Nathan. "It's the last one."

"Thanks," Nathan responded, as he pondered what to do.

50. Vacation with Pay

Phil was worried. As a junior counselor at eighteen, he was spending his first summer at camp. He had gone camping with his family when he was younger, but that was a very different kind of experience. Although his first few days as a counselor had been rather confusing, he liked the campers and the camp and was enjoying his work. Except for one problem, he would have been very happy.

Phil had been assigned to work in the same cabin as Zack, a senior counselor with several years of experience at the camp. Zack had just received his master's degree and planned to start a year-round job that fall. They liked each other immediately; Phil could easily see why Zack was one of the most popular people at camp. Recently, however, Phil had begun to notice that Zack somehow managed to disappear when there was work to be done, so Phil always seemed to end up handling the difficult assignments alone. In the morning, Zack stayed in bed until just before breakfast, and Phil had to see to it that the campers were ready. After breakfast, Zack usually didn't return to the cabin until cleanup was nearly completed. And so it went, all through the day.

Realizing that things were getting worse instead of better, Phil decided to express his concern. They happened to come in around the same time that night, and he saw an opportunity. "I've been a little upset the last week or so, Zack, and I thought you ought to know about it," he said. "We started out working so well together, but now I feel as if I'm carrying most of the load. You don't seem to be around very much."

Zack replied good-naturedly, "I guess you're right. I'm sorry. I'll watch it."

There was some improvement the next morning, but that afternoon Zack was nowhere to be found. Phil mentioned the problem again a few days later, and Zack's reaction was the same. He promised to do better, but there was no lasting change. After that, it did not take Phil long to figure out that Zack intended to get as much fun as he could out of his last summer at camp and was depending on his good reputation to cover up this year's deficiencies. He was still one of the best-liked people in camp. Meanwhile, Phil was carrying virtually the full burden of cabin responsibilities. He knew that the added strain was making him tired and short-tempered.

Phil finally decided that he and Zack would have to have a showdown. "Look, Zack, it's no use kidding ourselves anymore. You know you're not doing your share around here, and so do I. I'm tired of covering up for you all the time, too, especially since I'm doing all the work. Not only that, but the kids are suffering. You're not doing anything, and I'm getting too worn out to be much good to them, either."

Zack looked at him and shook his head. "I know I'm not doing much this year, and I'm sorry a kid as nice as you has to bear the brunt of it. It's my last year at camp — my last free summer. So I'm here to have a good time. But look at it this way — sure I'm taking it easy, but someday you'll get your chance, too."

51. A Conflict of Principles

Jim sat at the writing table in the counselors' cabin, trying to concentrate on a long overdue letter home. After the third try, he crumpled the papers he had been working on, threw them into the wastebasket, and walked outside. He stretched out in the cool grass in the shade of the building and twirled a blade of grass between his teeth.

It was Jim's first experience as a counselor, and he felt that he had done his job well. He had been pleased to learn, at the beginning of the season, that an older counselor who had spent many summers at various camps would be responsible for guiding and, in part, supervising him. Knowing that Duane would be there when unexpected problems arose gave him a feeling of security.

During the first few days, however, although Jim had been able to make it through, he had not felt that he had adequate control of the kids. No matter what he did, they seemed to have their own ideas about things and did what they wanted. There were no severe problems, but Jim felt that he was not fulfilling his role as a counselor.

It had not taken long for him to notice that Duane's way of doing things was vastly different from his. Almost immediately, Duane had established a pattern of military-like discipline and promoted the development of an intense feeling of exclusiveness within his group. Still, the group had quickly developed an enthusiastic spirit and seemed to stand out in everything. Jim admired that. Duane's group marched to the dining hall in an orderly line, and violations of rules were quickly and firmly dealt with.

But Jim gradually realized that Duane's group seemed to lose its discipline whenever Duane himself was absent. When Jim was called upon to handle Duane's group, he seemed unable to maintain control at all. Once or twice the group was left alone for a few minutes, and the result was complete chaos.

Duane, who was well liked and a leader among the staff, continued to advise him to tighten up on discipline with his boys and to try to develop a more competitive spirit toward other groups. Jim listened each time and tried to raise some other ideas, but Duane seemed to become more and more impatient with him. Increasingly, Jim found himself going to the directors themselves when he needed help.

Around the middle of the season, Jim caught a mild virus and was forced to spend two days in the infirmary. Duane helped to cover Jim's group during this time and, on Jim's return, he found the group restive and unhappy. They felt that Duane had been unfair and entirely too strict, and they were afraid that he was going to hit them.

Jim was determined to talk to Duane about it when they next met, but he was unprepared for Duane's enthusiastic greeting. "Jim, I sure whipped your misfits into shape for you, didn't I?" he said.

Startled, Jim stared at him for a moment and asked, "What do you mean?"

"They didn't have any respect for authority," he replied. "They didn't know what discipline means, and they had no spirit."

Jim got angry at this, and he told Duane about the complaints the campers had made. Duane laughed. "They're bigger babies than I thought," he said. "Kids have to be a little bit afraid, or else they don't respect us." Jim tried to dispute the point, but Duane just said, "You'll learn. You're too idealistic," and he walked away.

There must be a better way, Jim thought. I didn't come here to play policeman. But I don't know what to do.

52. Taking It Personally

The campers were playing softball, and the game was being delayed because two boys were arguing about whose turn it was to bat. Craig, the counselor, had not intervened because he hoped they would figure out a solution to their problem on their own. At the moment, it did not look promising.

"You're not up; I am!"

"No you're not. I batted after Rachel last time and Rachel just batted."

"You did not. I did. Rachel was tagged out at second when I hit. Remember?"

"No she wasn't."

"Yes,...."

"No, she was tagged out at third base when *I* batted."

"Let me finish! Rachel, come here and tell this faggot who it was that batted after you the last time."

"*You're* the fag...." At these last remarks, the two boys went down in a pile clutching and grabbing each other.

Clearly angry, Craig approached them and held them a little too tightly by their shoulders as he pulled them apart. "You guys know this isn't the way to solve problems," he said through clenched teeth. "Why do you think problems can be solved by fighting? Are you having a good time now? Isn't this fun? And calling someone a faggot is the wrong thing to say around me. Go back to the cabin and cool off until the rest of us are done playing." Craig sent them on their way and returned to the backstop muttering to himself.

Robbie, another counselor, approached him cautiously. "I've

never seen you so upset before, especially with those two. They're always arguing about something. This certainly isn't the first time, and you rarely even show frustration. Why did you make them leave the game instead of helping them work out a better way of solving the problem?"

"I don't know... I guess they just set me off."

"And what did you mean by 'calling someone a faggot is the wrong thing to say around me'? Why is that worse than any other name?"

Craig looked Robbie in the eyes. "I thought by now you knew I was gay. Calling him a faggot brought back too many bad memories. I'm just tired of it."

Stunned, Robbie struggled for something to say.

53. A Question of Judgment

Heather giggled as she looked over her shoulder to see if anyone was listening. "Can you believe that Gary peed so close to us?"

Kim laughed in disbelief. "No way. He was so casual, like it was no big deal. And when he realized that we had heard him, he just said, 'That's life in the woods!' He's been the tripping director too long. He needs to get back to civilization, back where humans live!"

"Unbelievable! It's not like we saw anything, but there's no way I'd pull down my pants in front of anybody. You don't see the deer out there calling attention to themselves."

Kim laughed again. "See you later. I have to stop off at the cabin to finish my letter home before dinner."

Tiffany, their counselor, had not gone on the hike with her group of eleven year olds that afternoon because it was her day off. Later that evening, just before bedtime, she stopped in to put her laundry away and overheard someone say something about Gary exposing himself. She quickly tuned in on the conversation.

"Yeah," Kim was saying, "isn't that what wolves do — pee around the boundaries of their territory so everyone will know it's theirs?"

Jessica chimed in. "It's just like a boy to want to show off that way. He should grow up a little."

"Boys are so gross," said Heather. "Maybe we should have done the same thing to see how he would like it!" The girls laughed, but Tiffany was troubled by the conversation and decided that it was a good time to change the subject. She sidetracked them by talking about the schedule for the next day.

The next morning, Tiffany approached Gary and told him about the campers' conversation. "I know that learning to deal with some of this stuff is part of being in the outdoors, Gary. But don't you think it would be a good idea to be more careful? What if one of the girls mentioned this incident to her parents? They might be a little suspicious, and the last thing we want is to have someone questioning our ethics."

Gary looked at her, wondering if she was questioning *his* ethics. "I didn't mean any harm," he said. "There were witnesses to what happened. It isn't like it was with one camper, and I was behind a bush. Basically, they heard it, but they didn't see anything."

"Gary, the fact that they were talking about it means that it still made an impression. Don't you understand that? Maybe *you* don't think you exposed yourself, but that's what the *campers* thought. If they say that around the wrong person, it could be trouble."

Gary thought for a minute. "But don't my intentions count for anything? Or the context? It *was* out in the woods."

"Yes, of course they do, but those things don't always get communicated when the girls are talking about something like this."

"Well, I find this whole discussion ridiculous. I can't control how people are going to perceive things. If they want to believe that there was something wrong going on, they're going to believe it no matter what I do or say. So I'm just going to keep doing what I think is best."

"Gary," Tiffany objected, wondering at the same time whether she might better get back to her group to deal with the situation there rather than wasting her breath with him, "…

54. When Is a Hug Not a Hug?

Darly watched as her twelve-year-old girls sprawled around Brian, the waterfront instructor. Two of them were sitting on his lap. Brian had been spending a significant amount of his free time with Darly's group. She appreciated that because it relieved some of the pressure on her, and it was nice to have another adult to talk to, even if it was only small talk. And he certainly had a way with her girls.

"Go get 'em, babe!" Brian said, as Gina left to play volleyball. As she walked away, he slapped her on the rear end in encouragement, and another girl took her place on Brian's lap.

As she watched, Darly had to admit to herself that she was uncomfortable. To be more specific, it was the physical contact between Brian and the girls, including the girls sitting on his lap, hugs, roughhousing, and kisses on the cheek. Darly wasn't sure why it bothered her, but she decided that she had better talk to Brian about it. After lunch, she caught him alone while he was getting ready to go to the lake. "Brian, can I talk to you for a minute?"

"Sure."

"I'm glad that you've been hanging out with us. You're a great help and the girls like you a lot. But I'm a little concerned about how *much* they like you and the amount of physical contact."

He stopped what he was doing and looked at her.

"They're very young and impressionable, and they might get the wrong idea. Other people who see it might, too. I like you to hang around, but let's cool it with the physical contact, okay?" Darly paused for a reaction.

Brian's face flushed. "Some people are so paranoid and defensive. Physical contact is normal, and people need it. Why is touching always interpreted as sexual?"

"The kind of touching and teasing that goes on between you and my girls is often done in a romantic way. When it's between boys and girls or men and girls, it's easily misinterpreted."

"By whom?"

"Anybody."

"You mean by you." Brian looked annoyed. "Look, if you don't want me to spend time with your girls, just say so! But don't accuse me of having devious interests in your kids. If you're not careful, your girls are going to learn that men can't be interested in them unless it's sexual. Think about it!"

"That's not what I mean!" Darly protested. "I'm not concerned about you," she lied. "I'm just worried about what other people might think."

"Really?" Brian looked skeptical. "I have to go to the lake now. Until we get this straightened out, I'll just stay away." He picked up his gear and walked out the door.

55. Shhh!

Although he was one of the older counselors, Dan had never been to camp before. Some of his friends, camping veterans, had convinced him to join them this summer, and he had taken to it like a duck to water.

One day, the head counselor, Ken, approached him. "Dan, you've been doing a great job. I have to go to town to take care of some things. Can you run the all-camp program this afternoon?"

"Sure!" beamed Dan.

As the afternoon progressed, Dan realized that the job wasn't so easy. In particular, he was having problems getting the kids quiet so that he could explain the activities. Okay, it's my first time in charge; I guess this is normal, he figured.

As the weeks passed, Ken had a few other occasions to ask Dan to run things, with similar results. It gradually dawned on him that part of the problem was that the other counselors were not helping to control the campers and, even worse, were often disruptive themselves by talking while he was trying to quiet things down. Dan decided to raise the issue at the next staff meeting.

"Yes, Ken, I have something," Dan responded at the meeting when Ken asked if anyone had anything else to bring up. "I've been noticing that each time I have to make an announcement at a large group activity, I have a really tough time getting the kids to listen. I've tried various things, but it feels like I'm really not getting much help." He looked around the room at his fellow counselors. "Rather than setting a good example, many of you guys are even the ones who are disrupting!"

"I haven't noticed any problem," Steve shot back. "Maybe you just need to command more attention!" Other staff members seemed to side more with Steve, but they agreed to make more of an effort.

The next week, Dan was put in charge again, and he had some announcements to make during lunch. While attempting to get things down to a low roar, he noticed Steve and Jack talking on the side while their campers ignored his pleas for quiet.

56. Resentment

Without the lights on, the staff cabin was dark, even in midafternoon on this cool, cloudy day. A few counselors were sprawled on the old armchairs and sofas, some sipping warm drinks and talking about their troubles.

"Yeah, my kids are a pain today. They won't listen to anything I tell them to do, and they aren't interested in doing anything else, either." Jackie rolled over so she could face the window.

"I know what you mean," said Dana. "I think all the kids have hit a midcamp slump. They act like this is a prison and we're the jailers. They're suffering so badly." Dana poked Shannon awake as she walked to the refrigerator. "What's going on with you?"

"Oh, nothing," yawned Shannon. "My kids are no different, but I'm more frustrated with Michelle. She's supposed to be our supervisor, but it seems like every time I need some help she's missing in action. Do you guys know where she goes?"

Dana agreed, without answering the question. "I know what you mean. Sometimes we're out there busting our butts in the hot sun and she's nowhere to be found. She isn't very supportive of counselors. Did you hear what she did to Sandy yesterday?" Dana continued without waiting for a response. "Sandy asked for some time off for today because her family is visiting. Michelle told her she couldn't, because supposedly we're short."

Shannon groaned. "Maybe, but Sandy doesn't get to see her parents very often. Why couldn't Michelle take Sandy's kids for a little while? She has an easy job; it wouldn't be that tough on her to actually work with kids again. Maybe she could demonstrate all those ideas she keeps telling us about, and we could see how they work with real kids."

Jackie jumped up. "Yeah, I remember when she was just a peon counselor like us. She wasn't always such a hotshot. I think she's forgotten how hard counselors have to work."

57. Union Rules?

Damon and Lamont lay sprawled on the grass in the late afternoon sunshine, feeling exhausted. This had been an especially busy week because they were responsible for planning an evening program for the entire camp in addition to their usual cabin group responsibilities. But now almost everything was ready, except that they needed more staff help.

Damon was talking about the waterfront staff's response to the request that they help out. "Can you believe those guys? All we asked was that they give us a hand for one evening. You wouldn't think that would be too much trouble, since they don't have anything else to do after dinner. It's not like it's a permanent arrangement! But the one time we ask for help, they say 'no.' Did they have a good excuse?"

"No," replied Lamont. "They just said that they had planned to get out of camp that evening."

"Well, we don't get regular nights off during sessions. Why should they?" Damom's voice was louder. "And they have a short workday. Swimming lessons don't start until ten-thirty, and open swim is over at four o'clock. They should have plenty of time to help the rest of us once in a while. Maybe counselors shouldn't bother to go to the beach with our kids," he continued. "Let the lifeguards take care of them during swim time."

Lamont agreed. "While they're working, they're busy putting on suntan lotion and turning their chairs so their bodies get just the right sun angle. It's not that difficult to sit there and watch kids swim, at least not as hard as being a counselor. Even when we're at the lake, we're expected to be in the water with the kids. We don't get that much easy work."

"The kitchen staff is the same way. They have to get up early, but they get long breaks between meals...."

"Damon," interrupted Lamont, "the bottom line is, what can we do about it?"

58. "What? Rick Has Been Fired?"

Word spread like wildfire among the staff. "You must be kidding!" someone said, but Rick affirmed the accuracy of the rumor to the group of counselors who had gathered near the cabins.

It was Rick's first season at camp, and he had been one of the most popular counselors with campers and staff almost since the day of his arrival. He was also one of the youngest. His own group of boys idolized him, and his charisma and humor seemed vital to the morale of the staff as well.

Gradually, the counselors' surprise gave way to feelings of anger and resentment. Many wanted the entire staff to quit in protest, but cooler heads suggested that they get more information before taking drastic action that they might regret later. They asked Rick to explain what had happened.

"As some of you know, I conducted a kind of a séance with the kids a couple of nights ago," he began. "It was mostly a joke, and they had a good time pretending they were contacting the dead. No big deal. But somehow Val found out about it, and this morning she and Gary told me that I had to go." Val was the camp director and Gary, as head of the intermediate boys' unit, was Rick's supervisor. "We talked all morning, but they wouldn't budge. I think Gary's happy about it. I've never felt that he liked me. He acts like he's jealous of me for some reason."

"Look, Val can't do that to you," interjected Sam. "Let's go down and ask her to give you another chance. If she won't be reasonable, we'll all threaten to quit! Does anybody disagree with that?" No one appeared to, so Sam continued. "Okay, here's a plan. Let's choose three or four of us to go to Val. They can represent the rest of us."

"How about you, Sam?" said someone. "And Laura," said another.

"I'd like Mitch to go," said Sam. "He's rational, but firm. He ought to do the talking." Hearing no objections from Mitch or the group, he continued. "This is a good time to go, since it's rest period and the kids are in the cabins. Will the rest of you keep an eye on our groups?"

Fortunately, Val was available in her office. "Come in," she said. "What can I help you with?"

Mitch glanced sideways at Sam, who nodded at him to begin. "You probably know why we're here. We heard that Rick was asked to leave, and we're not very happy about it. His kids like him, the staff likes him, and we thought the administration liked him, too. We want to hear from you why he is being fired."

"I can put it simply," she said. "The immediate cause was learning that Rick conducted a séance with his boys. Doing so is hazardous and completely unethical professionally. It's also contradictory to the mission of our camp. It sends wrong messages to the children about what their interests should be and what spirituality is about. What could Rick have been thinking? Remember, we're taking care of other people's children."

"But it was a joke, Val," said Mitch. "He didn't mean anything by it. The kids were talking about being scared of the dark after their night hike, and someone said something about spirits. So Rick thought it would be fun to pretend they were communicating with the spirits in the dark — kind of like a creative ghost story.

"That may be true," replied Val, "but it doesn't make it right — or safe. And it's not what the campers thought. Did you know that some of them were quite upset and frightened? Did you know that three of them spent last night in the infirmary because they were so frightened? Did you know that some of the boys are still convinced that they talked to the dead?"

There was an embarrassed silence, but Sam jumped into the breach. "Frankly, Val," he said, "there are other things that concern us as well. It looks like Gary wanted Rick fired because he was jealous of Rick's popularity. Isn't it possible that this séance business is being blown out of proportion as an excuse?"

"I just told you why Rick was fired," responded Val, beginning to get annoyed. "It was my decision, not Gary's, and this isn't the only incident that I find problematic. Maybe one of the reasons that the kids like him so much is that he does things at the expense of what we stand for to build himself up in their eyes. I have spoken to him about this before."

"Val, it's not only the campers who like Rick," responded Sam. "The staff looks to him for leadership as well, and he contributes so much to our camp spirit that...."

Just then, Sam was interrupted by a loud chant coming from the direction of the camper's cabins. "We want Rick! We want Rick! We want Rick!" Val smiled as the counselors' committee watched in genuine surprise. Sam cursed under his breath, realizing that the counselors must have organized a camper protest march that could only harm their cause. Slowly, the campers came into sight, marching and still chanting, "We want Rick! We want Rick! We want Rick!"

Obviously caught off stride and embarrassed, Sam finally spoke again. "Val, believe me, we didn't know anything about this. I've never been so surprised in my life. I'll go and get them to stop."

Val laughed. "Don't be surprised. I'm not. Some of the other counselors probably decided to organize a minor revolt. Kids'll go along with something dramatic like that very easily. I'm sure that half of them don't even know Rick very well."

Mitch looked annoyed. "Val," he said, "don't use this as another excuse for not reinstating Rick. Let's ignore those kids and stick to the issue. I can assure you that if Rick is reinstated, the counselors will make certain that the kids don't pull anything like this again. That's a promise." The other counselors nodded their agreement.

"That doesn't change what happened. We didn't want to lose Rick, but he really gave us no choice."

"Then you're telling us that you won't consider reinstating him?" asked Laura.

"Yes. I don't see how I can, even without the demonstration the kids just put on. Don't you see what that would be teaching them?"

"Look, Val," Laura said earnestly, "this staff needs Rick. Can't he even be reinstated on a trial basis, just for a few days? See how he does, then we'll accept whatever decision you think best. You know he's valuable."

"It just can't be done, Laura," Val said. "I'm sorry that you can't see the importance of all these things and their impact on the kids, but Rick will have to go."

Sam and Laura looked at Mitch, waiting for him to speak. "That's final?" asked Sam after a long pause.

"Yes," replied Val, "and I think we'd better get back to the campers and try to calm them down."

The counselors were clearly very annoyed. "Wait a minute," Sam said firmly in a slow, measured tone, looking directly at Mitch. "I think Mitch has something to add, don't you, Mitch?" Mitch gazed at the hostile eyes of his fellow counselors as Val settled back to hear what he was going to say.

Working with Parents

59. Trial by Fury

Sandy looked back on the first week of camp with great satisfaction. She had been a little worried because most of the group of young teenagers in her cabin were experienced campers and this was her first season. But everything seemed to be going well, and Sandy was glad that she had been given this particular group.

The director, Jordan, had told her about them at her interview, after Sandy had been hired, and had asked her if she would like to be their counselor. Most of the girls in the group had been cabinmates for two or three seasons, and they had had the same counselor the past two years. "She's not coming back, and we're looking to replace her with someone who will carry on with the really unique program that she and her girls have started."

He had gone on to describe how, three years before, the group had started to build a campsite. They had continued to work on it each summer, and last year they had actually laid the foundation and most of the floor and erected part of the walls of a cabin to serve as a storage area and rainy-day kitchen. They had even built a stone fireplace and chimney into one of the walls. The program had sounded exciting to Sandy, and she had jumped at the opportunity to become a part of it. Not only did she think it would be fun, but she saw it as a very worthwhile experience for the girls in the group as well.

The experienced campers had arrived at camp full of enthusiasm and had wasted no time in telling the three new girls about their ongoing project. Two of the newcomers had accepted it with a spirit that matched Sandy's own, while the third, Janie, had hardly reacted at all.

Right after dinner the first night, the group had gone to see how the winter had treated their work and to show it to Sandy and the new girls. The wood of the partially built cabin had been covered for the winter and was in good condition. After inspecting it carefully, they had lighted a campfire and gathered around to plan the next steps. They had decided that they should first complete the walls and put on the roof.

The next step would be to build a permanent latrine; then they could move out to the site and put the finishing touches on the inside of the cabin. They had planned to work only mornings at the beginning. All in all, Sandy had felt that they were planning realistically and well. Except for Janie, the new girls had become fully involved and had even contributed some new ideas that were accepted by the group.

Now it was a week later, and the work had proceeded even more rapidly than they had expected. Some of the girls were finishing up the roof, while the others were already laying the foundation for the latrine, all under the caretaker's guidance. Soon they would be able to live there, and as the time grew near their excitement goaded them into working even more quickly. They were spending just about every morning and some afternoons at the site.

That afternoon, as the group returned to the main camp, they saw a man and a woman near the entrance. "It's my mom and dad!" shouted Janie in apparent surprise, as she ran toward them. After the Bauers greeted their daughter, she brought them over to meet Sandy.

"Hello, Mr. and Mrs. Bauer," said Sandy. "Seeing you is a nice surprise."

"Hello," responded Mr. Bauer, and Sandy could see that he and his wife were not friendly. "We wanted to see you and to find out what's going on here."

"What do you mean?"

"Janie has been writing us that the camp is making her build cabins and latrines," replied Mrs. Bauer. "We sent her to camp to have fun, not to be a carpenter!"

Sandy was taken aback. "But you don't understand," she said. "This is a project the girls want to do. They chose it themselves, and look at the experience they're getting, working with their hands and contributing something worthwhile to their camp at the same time. Besides, they *are* having fun."

"We don't fall for that nonsense," sneered Mrs. Bauer. "It's just the camp's way of getting work done without paying for the labor. She's just a child and, besides, we're not paying good money for her to work! Aren't there child labor laws about things like this?"

"But she's not..." began Sandy, until Mr. Bauer interrupted.

"We don't want to discuss it any further," he said. "Just see to it that our daughter has a decent program from now on. And no more forced labor, or we'll just pull her out!"

60. In Loco Parentis

After delivering twelve-year-old Trevor to camp and getting his things put away, Mr. and Mrs. Jacobson asked to speak with Graham, his counselor, before they left. "Now, we want to make sure that you understand everything that Trevor needs," his father said.

"Sure, Mr. Jacobson." Graham sensed that trouble was coming, but he put on a serviceable smile.

"You understand that Trevor's wheelchair is not a toy and that the other boys shouldn't play with it."

"Yes, of course." Graham hoped that his annoyance with their condescending attitude didn't show.

"We also want to make sure that you remember to take Graham to the nurse on time to get his medicine. He can usually dress himself, but he has trouble with buttons and with his shoes. He can also transfer himself in and out of the chair, but someone should always be nearby in case he has a problem. He is fussy about what he eats, so if he won't eat the food on the menu, something else should be provided." Graham nodded. Except for the menu, most of their requests were reasonable, even if their tone was demanding.

"Trevor has sunblock in his suitcase, and you should make sure he uses it every day, because his light skin burns easily. He also gets rashes from bug bites, so please make sure he uses his insect repellant before you go into the woods or anyplace where he might get bitten."

Graham kept his thoughts to himself. "Well, we'll take good care of him," he responded, "and I'm sure he'll have a good time."

"Don't forget his medicine, and make sure he calls us every day."

"All right, we'll see you next week." Relieved that the conversation was over, Graham walked back toward the cabin.

The next four days passed without incident, and Graham thought that Trevor, while somewhat timid, was fitting in well. The other boys were cheerfully helping him out when necessary.

At the end of the fourth day, Karen, the head counselor, stopped by. "Mr. Jacobson called and expressed concern about Trevor's health. Trevor told them that he had been on a hike and had been bitten by several mosquitos. I assured him that I would check on it, but that they were probably the normal bites that everyone gets." Together they walked to the cabin and Trevor came to the door.

"Hi, Trevor," Karen said. "How's it going?"

"Great. Today we went on a hike to the point and swam all afternoon."

"That's nice," replied Karen, as she looked him over. "Are you feeling all right?"

"Sure, why wouldn't I be?"

"No reason, just checking. See you later."

The following Wednesday was visiting day for parents, and the Jacobsons spent two hours eating with Trevor and touring the camp. After most of the visitors had left, Karen found Graham playing ball with several of the boys in his group and called him aside. "The Jacobsons are worried about Trevor," she said. "They claim that he is sunburned even though they gave you instructions about using sunblock. They want to talk to you about it in my office."

"He's just a little pink, like most light-skinned campers get. Do they want him to spend all his time indoors?" Graham felt his frustration growing as they walked toward the office.

Appendix

Supplementary Questions

Case 1: Virtual Kid

1. Should Jordan focus his effort on Sam or on the other boys? Why? Does he have to make a choice? Why or why not?

2. What are some good ways of coping with high-energy campers?

3. Is "making it easier" a good motivation for removing a problem child from a cabin group? Why or why not? How does one decide when it is best?

4. What should be the criteria for deciding when a child should not be at camp?

Case 2: Sideline Sally

1. Why does Nina consider Sally to be a problem? Should she? Why or why not?

2. Are there likely to be underlying reasons for Sally's behavior? What might they be? Does it make a difference if there are? If so, how?

3. What should Nina's goals or criteria for success with Sally be? Why?

Case 3: Boo-Boo. Boo Hoo?

1. Is telling ghost stories appropriate, given the goals of being at camp — an environment that may be novel — and being away from family?

2. Does the age of the camper make a difference, and are some kinds of stories more acceptable than others? If so, what kinds, and why?

3. Is there anything Dominick can do to resolve Jamie's fears? If so, what?

4. What are the values of storytelling at camp, and how can they best be achieved?

Case 4: A Contest of Wills

1. Is the rule reasonable? Why or why not?

2. What risks were entailed in the method Alice used to try to get Erin to finish eating?

3. When should group pressure be used on an individual camper and when should it not be used? Why? Why did Alice's attempt to use it backfire?

4. How should Alice extricate herself from this situation? Why?

Case 5: It Takes Two to Tangle

1. What are the interrelated problems in this case? Can they be separated for purposes of discussion? Should they be? Why or why not?

2. Why did Toby react so violently to the way Bobby controlled the group? To what extent should a counselor permit himself to become emotionally involved with his campers? Why?

3. Is smoking a serious behavior problem? Why or why not? What is the difference between serious problems and nonserious problems?

4. Is obedience the most important issue here? Why or why not?

Case 6: Like Night and Day

1. When should a counselor be particularly alert for signs of home-sickness? What are some of the things to watch for?

2. What should a counselor do for a homesick child? Why? Can trying to help make things worse? Why and how?

3. What should counselors avoid doing with campers who are homesick? Why?

4. Is limiting parental contact a good idea? Why or why not? What circumstances should be considered in this connection?

5. Why did Patty say, "*Maybe you're right.* Maybe I should just go home...?" What implications are there in this for the counselor?

Case 7: It's Not Fair

1. What are the dangers of giving too much attention to children who act out?

2. Should a counselor admit being at fault and apologize to a camper or campers in a situation like this? Why or why not? If so, how?

3. Is there any way for Sheila to meet Jennifer's needs and those of the rest of the group simultaneously? If so, how?

4. How can Sheila acknowledge her mistake in a situation such as this, if she decides to do so, without making things more difficult for either of the girls?

Case 8: The Acid Test

1. What are the safety implications of what Lance did? The educational implications? The emotional implications for Dan?

2. Should Matt report what has happened? Why or why not? If so, to whom?

3. What should Matt tell Dan? Why?

Case 9: Fact or Fiction

1. How might Marcus's relationship with Corey be affected by Corey's actions?

2. What specific actions should Marcus take now?

3. What might be the reasons for Corey's behavior?

Case 10: For Love or Money

1. Should Kevin have taken the money when he found it? Why or why not? Does the fact that he did so complicate the effort to solve the problem? If so, how?

2. How much evidence do you need to suspect someone of stealing?

3. What should be done now? Is talking to Johnny likely to be effective? Why or why not?

4. When children steal, what are some likely reasons? If Johnny stole the money, why might he have hidden it in such an obvious place?

Case 11: On the Home Front

1. Should Erica say anything to Danielle about her parents? Why or why not? If so, what should she say?

2. What kind of assumptions do we often make about young people who are quiet and withdrawn?

3. What other behaviors might be typical of children whose families are having difficulties? How should one respond?

Case 12: I Wanna Hold Your Hand

1. Should Drew's behavior be considered unusual or strange? How might it be interpreted?

2. What other types of situations might lead to similar reactions on the part of counselors? Is it possible to avoid reacting instinctively to such situations? If so, how?

3. What are Keith's options now?

Case 13: Misplaced Trust

1. What is Derrick's dilemma?

2. What are his special legal and moral responsibilities, if any, in connection with this incident?

3. What might be the consequences for Bobby during the next few days? After he goes home? In that light, what should Derrick say or do now?

4. What might be the consequences for the other campers? How should Derrick deal with those?

Case 14: For the Sake of Appearances

1. What problems are imminent for Tara? How can Marie help her face and meet them?

2. What should Marie's goals be with respect to Mrs. Ellwood? How should she respond to Mrs. Ellwood's letter, or should the director answer it? If the latter, how?

3. Does Marie have any kind of moral obligation to Ronnie? Does the camp administration? If so, what?

4. Should Marie have taken any action earlier? Why or why not? If so, what?

5. In most camps, there is some opportunity for teenagers to form close boy-girl relationships with partners of a different race, religion, economic status, or other such group — relationships that would perhaps be much more difficult at home. In such cases, what is a camp's responsibility to the teenagers themselves, to their parents, and to society?

Case 15: Where Do We Go from Here?

1. Is Christy being too critical of the other girls? If so, in what sense, and how should her counselor respond? Why?

2. Were her expectations of camp fair and reasonable ones? Why or why not?

3. What are the values of highlighting community service as a significant camp program component? What should determine whether such service is focused on the camp community itself or on the world outside? What kinds of service should be involved? Why?

Case 16: Disability Equals Dumb?

1. When campers treat each other unjustly, can counselors do anything about it? If so, what?

2. Should Maria talk to Carmen, the other campers, or to both? Why or why not?

3. Should Maria focus on convincing the campers that Carmen isn't dumb or on the unfairness of their treatment of her? Why?

Case 17: Hurling Hailey

1. Is it proper for camp staff to intervene in a long-term problem such as this that does not impinge directly or seriously on the program or on other campers? Why or why not?

2. Does Hailey have a right to privacy in this regard? Why or why not? In that light, was Renee's visit to the nurse appropriate? What about her request that it be kept confidential? Why or why not?

3. Should Renee now discuss the situation and her plans with her supervisor? Why or why not?

4. Is contacting Hailey's parents appropriate and likely to be effective? Why or why not?

5. How should questions asked by the other girls about Hailey's problem be handled? Why?

Case 18: A Case of Chaos

1. What might have been the underlying cause of this episode? Why did it explode at this particular time?

2. What is the role of routines at camp? How can routines best be established?

3. In what other situations may the phenomenon of behavior contagion operate among children at camp? How can it best be handled? In what situations may behavior contagion operate among staff members?

4. Should counselors be very strict for the first few days to show them who's boss? Why or why not? What assumptions are implicit in this approach?

Case 19: The Squeaky Wheel Gets the Grease

1. Is it a good idea to "negotiate" a solution in the way that George did in a situation like this? Why or why not? Should such an offer be viewed as bribery for good behavior? Why or why not?

2. How might George plan so that he can meet the more immediate needs of the two subgroups as well as bring them closer together over time?

3. What are the values of group discussions in working with campers? How frequently should they be held? Should they be scheduled in advance or as needed? If the latter, how should "need" be determined?

Case 20: "The Best Laid Plans..."

1. Do practical jokes, such as the one mentioned in this case, belong at camp? What are their values and their disadvantages? Who is usually the victim?

2. Do you agree with Bobbie's statement that "it's a sign that something's wrong when a group becomes exclusive and self-centered, no matter how good its spirit may seem in other ways?" Why or why not?

3. What is the wider significance of exclusiveness and scapegoating on the part of a group? If this behavior is accepted without comment, what might the members of the group be learning? Should it be combatted? If so, how?

Case 21: Democracy in Action

1. In what ways and to what degree, if any, should campers participate in planning the program? Why? What does participation in planning mean? What problems does this raise? How should they be handled?

2. Does democratic decision making mean absolute majority rule? Is the concept of democracy applicable here? Why or why not? If so, how should it be defined?

3. What are some alternative decision-making procedures and their advantages and disadvantages?

4. How should program decisions like this one be made? Should campers be permitted to spend their time arguing, as in this case, rather than participating in activities? Why or why not?

5. Can a situation like this be used as an educational opportunity? If so, how?

Case 22: Readiness, Leadership, and Democracy

1. Should a camp have a campers' council? Why or why not? If so, what should its functions be? What areas, if any, should it avoid? Why?

2. What should the concepts of democracy and camper leadership at camp imply? What should they not imply? Why? How can this best be communicated to campers?

3. What could Keri have done to guide the experience more effectively?

4. How can a counselor best use camper decision making as a teaching tool?

Case 23: Food for Thought

1. Should it be Rose's prerogative to make this decision? Why or why not?

2. Should Kelly accept the decision? Why or why not? What are her alternatives?

3. Should it have been necessary for Kelly to check with Rose in advance, in view of the "two days' notice" regulation? Why or why not? If not, should she have done so anyway? If so, why?

4. How could Rose have made her special problem into a learning experience for Kelly's campers? How could Kelly do so after her campers have been rebuffed by Rose?

Case 24: Is My Face Red?

1. How can counselors best react when campers tell dirty jokes in their presence? What difference, if any, do the age of the camper and the situation make? What other factors should be considered?

2. What should a counselor do when he or she is in a position to criticize another staff member's behavior? Suppose the counselor feels that he or she must do so to maintain credibility with the campers.

3. What should a counselor do if it becomes apparent that he or she has indirectly and inadvertently criticized the behavior of a colleague, as in this case? What advantages and disadvantages might there be in trying to ignore or overlook the situation? In trying to backtrack?

4. Does ignoring or overlooking something the campers do or say indicate approval? Why or why not?

Case 25: A Child with a Difference

1. What are some reasons why children wet their beds?

2. What are other possible reasons why Jared had never been to camp before? Why might it be important to look for other reasons? What are the risks involved in attempting to do this?

3. Might there have been better ways to handle this situation? If so, what are they?

4. What kinds of special needs are likely to be encountered at camp? Should children who have special needs be accepted as campers? Why or why not? What are the obligations of the counselor in such situations?

Case 26: Believe It or Not

1. Denise doesn't know what really happened. How do you handle conflicting claims in situations like this? Is it likely that you would ever find out the truth?

2. Even if she never learns the truth, is there anything she can do to turn it into an educational experience for the campers? If so, how?

3. When should a counselor refuse to get involved in camper conflicts and when is it best to intervene? Why?

Case 27: A Rude Awakening

1. Is Geoff's reasoning correct that the food wasn't really stolen? Why or why not? If not, how would you refute it?

2. Was Wade justified in opening campers' bags? Why or why not? How does he defend his actions to the campers?

3. What does the case imply about Wade's relationships with his campers? Why was he so sure that they were not guilty when David accused them?

4. What would you encourage a camper to do if he knew that some members of his cabin group had stolen the food? When is it tattling and when is it being a good citizen?

5. What is the broader problem with Reggie and how would you deal with it? What about Geoff and Damian? And the rest of the group?

Case 28: Caught in the Act!

1. What are the most likely implications of what occurred? How serious is it? What should be done about it?

2. To what extent and in what way should a counselor attempt to handle a situation that arises in another counselor's group when the other counselor is away? What factors should be taken into account in making such a decision?

Case 29: Just for Fun

1. Is there a problem here? If so, is it primarily a sexual issue, or is it more general?

2. Is it important to intervene? If so, how? Is it likely that Marty would have a useful effect on the boys' opinions and choices if he did intervene?

3. What ethical principles are relevant here?

4. What limits, if any, should camps place on sexual expression by teenagers? Why?

5. How should any such limits be established and enforced? Why?

Case 30: Sex and the Single Counselor

1. Assume that the true answer to Vanessa's questions is yes. Is it better to mislead the campers, not to answer at all, or simply to tell the truth? Why? Suppose the true answer is no, and consider these questions again.

2. What might be behind Vanessa's questions? Should this influence Wendy's response? If so, how?

3. What would you want the campers to gain from this discussion?

4. What would you do if you were Wendy? Why?

5. What are some other topics that might make staff members squirm? How would you deal with them?

Case 31: Just Kidding?

1. At what point does kidding become inappropriate? Is it ever appropriate? Does the topic — ethnicity, for example — make a difference? Why or why not?

2. Does the use of racial epithets necessarily mean that the boys are prejudiced? Why or why not?

3. Does Devon's race make a difference in the way he should respond? What should his objectives be when he intervenes?

Case 32: Truth or Consequences

1. Which view do you agree with? Why?

2. Should control of campers be a counselor's goal? Why or why not?

3. Why do you think campers behave or misbehave?

Case 33: What Price Efficiency?

1. What dangers, if any, are there in an attempt to deal with intragroup conflict by setting up intergroup rivalry or competition? Is Nate's war analogy valid? Why or why not? If so, what are the educational implications of Brett's proposal?

2. Should threats and/or punishment be used to enforce cleanup standards? Why or why not?

3. Might an award for all groups that meet a set cleanup standard be a healthy motivating device? Why or why not? Would this be artificial and/or objectionable? Why or why not?

4. What should the role (or roles) of the cabin counselor be during cleanup? Why?

5. Did the director handle the situation well? In what way? Might it have been handled more effectively? If so, how?

Case 34: After Dark

1. What are some possible explanations for the boys' unruly behavior? Is it possible for Anthony to do anything about it? If so, what?

2. Is their behavior really a problem? Why or why not?

Case 35: When Standards Conflict

1. To what extent should camp staff be concerned with campers' activity choices? Why? Should campers really have the choice to do what they want — even if it's nothing? Why or why not — and when?

2. What are the likely consequences of an attempt to force the campers to try new things?

3. Are there other strategies that Ruby could try? If so, what are they?

4. How much of the "real world" should be allowed at camp? Why? Should fashion magazines be banned? Radios? Video games? Racy novels? Why or why not?

Case 36: In the Face of Adversity

1. What are the risks and benefits of the way Lynne motivated her girls to accept the overnight? How else could she have done it?

2. What choice should Lynne make *now* to increase the possibility that they will want to go camping again? Or does she have a choice?

3. Is staying the rest of the night important? Why or why not?

4. What should Lynne do regarding the incident after the group gets back to its regular routine at camp? Why?

Case 37: An Ambitious Project

1. Should Alan have simply accepted his campers' original decision to build another fireplace? Why or why not?

2. In trying to plan cooperatively with a group of campers, how can a counselor encourage them to explore their dreams without implicit approval of impossible projects?

3. If Alan decides not to go ahead with the houseboat, should he tell the campers that the caretaker or the director (rather than Alan himself) made the decision? Why or why not?

4. What are the dangers of saying "no" to the project? Are there any alternatives? If so, what are they?

Case 38: Their True Colors?

1. What are the potential values of setting up broad competitive programs at camp? What are the risks?

2. Considering these factors, under what circumstances are such programs justified and when are they not? Why?

3. What is the appropriate role for counselors in such programs? Why? How can the benefits of having counselors involved on one side or another to help enhance each team's performance be balanced against the resulting risks?

Case 39: Bogged Down?

1. What is the critical conflict here? What difference does it make what they finally do?

2. What values would be reflected if they decided to go on the bog walk? If they decided not to go? Should the fact that they are late already and had to be reminded enter into the decision? Why or why not?

3. Would they enjoy and learn from the bog walk if they went? How would Scott feel if they didn't? Should either of these be a factor in making the decision? If so, how should these factors be assessed?

4. Would postponing the bog walk be a reasonable option? Why or why not?

5. Who should make the final decision? Why?

Case 40: Tradition!

1. Are there "compulsory" traditions at your camp that are difficult to explain? What are the rationales for them? How should counselors respond to them? Why?

2. It is likely that Evie will ever convince them? Why or why not? Should she try? Why or why not?

3. If so, are there other arguments she should use? If there are, what might they be?

4. What opportunities and dangers are there in being drawn into such a discussion?

Case 41: Beyond Belief?

1. Should a camp have the right to have a religious or other ideology? Why or why not? If so, how can the ideology be maintained without violating the rights of staff and campers?

2. Should campers have the right to choose whether to abide by the camp ideology? Why or why not? What about members of the staff? Why?

3. What are the advantages of having an ideologically homogeneous camp population vs. greater diversity? How can some of the values of diversity be achieved despite a relatively homogeneous camp population?

4. What are the potential spiritual values of camping and how can they best be achieved?

Case 42: The Role of a Leader

1. What should a counselor do if campers reveal that they have planned something intended as good fun, but against camp policy or likely to result in trouble? What should be done if he or she finds out accidentally, by overhearing campers planning it? Why?

2. Is there any way to be the "good guy" without approving? How important is it to be a good guy?

3. Is it important that all the adults in camp — counselors, directors, and others — maintain and enforce the same general limits on camper behavior? Why or why not?

4. Under what circumstances, if any, would a counselor be justified in accepting and hiding camper behavior that both the counselor and campers know is contrary to established camp regulations or policy? Why?

5. Graham sees this as an issue of a choice between being a counselor or a camper. Nick sees it as an issue of being liked and trusted. Are there other ways of thinking about the situation that might be more effective?

Case 43: Do It or Else!

1. Other then telling them to stop, what might Paul have done before or after the group arrived at the waterfront to avoid this situation?

2. What should Paul do now? Why?

3. Did Jack play an appropriate role? What should Jack do now? Why?

4. What are the pros and cons of using ultimatums to control camper behavior?

Case 44: Let's Talk

1. How can a counselor tell whether he or she is really meeting a camper's needs or is being used or manipulated in the service of other purposes? If convinced that the latter is the case, what should the counselor do? Why?

2. Other than to avoid doing something that they would rather not do, why might campers seek to manipulate counselors in this way?

3. Should a counselor always try to "be there" for the campers in his or her group? Why or why not? What about for campers in other groups? Why or why not? If not, how should counselors respond when they are approached for help by campers from other groups?

Case 45: A Touching Story

1. How would the situation be affected, if at all, if the counselor were female? If the camper were female? If both were female? Why?

2. What is the proper place for physical contact in working with young people of various ages in a camp setting?

3. What is your camp's policy on physical contact?

4. If you feel that the existing policy is not consistent with what is needed for the healthy development of the campers, how can the situation best be handled?

Case 46: What Can I Say?

1. Are the young teenagers in this case expressing primarily their resentment against the rules? What else might they be expressing? What are the implications of this for handling the case?

2. How should a counselor handle a situation in which his or her own opinions are in conflict with those of the camp administration or other camp staff? Why? What is the counselor's responsibility in such a situation? Why?

3. How should a counselor react when campers come to him with criticisms of another staff member? What alternatives are there other than simply to agree or disagree?

4. Should Brad attempt to interpret to the campers Tom's reason for being so insistent and emotional about the new rules? What are the potential risks and benefits either way?

Case 47: Going to Pot

1. Is Vic's response fair? Why or why not?

2. Does good behavior in one area compensate for problems in another? If so, under what conditions?

3. What behaviors are nonnegotiable? Why?

4. What are some of the things Laura might do that could be harmful to the camp? What are some that could be helpful?

5. Discuss the element of professional responsibility in the context of this case.

Case 48: Local Yokels

1. Is the problem only Jenny's and Claire's responsibility, or should someone else, like the camp director, get involved?

2. When is it a good idea to invite community residents onto the campgrounds and when is it not? Why?

3. What should be the relationship between a counselor's professional and private lives while working at camp? Why?

4. What are the legal implications of the situation portrayed in this case?

Case 49: Out of Bounds

1. What are the obligations of camp staff to uphold camp rules during off-duty times and at off-site locations?

2. What purpose does a rule against drinking serve?

3. Does it make a difference that some of the drinkers were underage?

4. What role do lifestyle standards play in the camp community?

5. What other issues might create similar problems?

Case 50: Vacation with Pay

1. When a counselor does not give his best effort, what are the likely effects on campers? On other counselors? On the administration? On the camp? On the counselor himself or herself?

2. What are some reasons why a counselor might not give his or her best effort?

3. Is Phil's approach likely to be effective? What are other ways of solving this problem, and how effective are they likely to be? Why?

Case 51: A Conflict of Principles

1. What should a counselor *say* to campers making obviously valid criticisms of another counselor or a supervisor? Why?

2. What *action*, if any, should a counselor take in response to an obviously valid criticism of another counselor or supervisor made by campers? Why?

3. How can control and discipline be managed most effectively?

Case 52: Taking It Personally

1. Should Craig's admission make a difference to Robbie? Why or why not? Is it relevant to their work? If so, how?

2. If Robbie has difficulty on a personal level with this new information, what should he do about it? Why?

3. What other personal issues can influence how we respond to children? How should we try to handle them? Why?

Case 53: A Question of Judgment

1. Should Tiffany try to ascertain what the girls actually saw and what they inferred from what they heard? Why or why not? In general, how important are appearances in situations like this? Why?

2. Should Tiffany tell anyone else about this situation? If so, who? What are the advantages or disadvantages of telling? Of not telling?

3. Assuming that Gary's story is accurate, were his actions appropriate? Why or why not? Should male counselors lead activities such as a one-day hike out of camp for a group of girls without a female counselor along? Why or why not? What about with a mixed group, or a female counselor with a group of boys?

4. Was it appropriate for Tiffany to avoid pursuing the discussion with the girls by changing the subject? Why or why not? Was the fact that she was on her day off a legitimate consideration in her actions? Why or why not? If so, how should it have been handled?

5. What are some other kinds of situations that arise in camp life that could be misinterpreted, and how can they best be handled?

Case 54: When Is a Hug Not a Hug?

1. What role should physical affection — such as touching, holding hands, and hugging as well as campers sitting on counselors' laps — play in camp life? Why?

2. What makes touching inappropriate? Age? Gender? Intent? Other factors? What are appropriate guidelines?

3. Is Darly's concern justified? Why or why not?

4. Is Brian's rationale for his actions acceptable? Why or why not?

5. What should counselors be aware of with regard to sexual abuse and harassment and possible allegations thereof?

Case 55: Shhh!

1. Should Dan have said something to the counselors when he became aware that they were not helping or even inadvertently obstructing his efforts to address the campers? Why or why not? If so, what might have been appropriate for him to say to them in front of the campers? Why?

2. What are some methods that can be used to address large groups of campers effectively, such as in making announcements and in speaking to them at greater length?

3. Would it be better to try to avoid situations where the campers must be spoken to in large groups? Why or why not? If so, what are some alternative approaches to transmitting needed information? What are the values, if any, of all-camp or other large group sessions?

Case 56: Resentment

1. What are the likely causes of the resentment that the counselors feel?

2. What would be some constructive and destructive ways for them to resolve the situation?

3. Are these types of misunderstandings between supervisors and counselors inevitable? If so, why?

4. What can a supervisor do to reduce frustration and resentment? What can the counselors do?

5. Why are counselors susceptible to this kind of conversation?

Case 57: Union Rules?

1. What might be the lifeguards' perspective on the situation? Why?

2. Is it important to build connections between program areas? Why or why not? If it is, what are some ways in which it can be done most effectively?

Case 58: What? Rick Has Been Fired?

1. How do you decide when to trust the camp administration's decisions, especially when they contradict your or a fellow staff person's point of view?

2. What are the dangers in using such an aggressive strategy to try to change the administration's position? When might it be appropriate?

3. Is it ethically appropriate for Val to discuss the situation with other counselors?

4. Is it ever appropriate to involve campers in staff disputes?

Case 59: Trial by Fury

1. Is the Bauers' complaint justified? Why or why not?

2. What is the proper role of work in camp life?

3. What is the difference between work and recreation at camp?

4. What choices does Sandy have now? What should she do?

Case 60: In Loco Parentis

1. What should Graham say to Trevor's parents? Why?

2. What should he say to Karen on the way to her office? Why?

3. Should Graham have said anything to the Jacobsons before this to try to prevent the problem? If so, what?

4. Are Trevor's parents' requests unreasonable? Why or why not? What might be other reasons for their behavior?

5. Are parents' expectations and children's best interests always the same? If not, how should counselors assign priorities among them? How can they best interpret this to all concerned?

Index to Cases

Note: the numbers here are case numbers, not page numbers. See the table of contents for brief case descriptions.

About the Authors

Jerry Beker, the father of the concept that underlies this book, holds a doctorate in youth guidance from Teachers College, Columbia University, and has been working in camping and youth service education for over 40 years. He was a camper through the 1940s and a counselor, unit supervisor, and program director during most of the '50s. Since then, Jerry has written extensively on youth welfare and development — he edits two journals in the field — and has held positions at a number of universities and youth serving agencies. He served over ten years as director of the Center for Youth Development and Research at the University of Minnesota, where he is currently Professor of Youth Studies in the School of Social Work. Jerry comes from a camp family. His father (and David's grandfather), Harold Beker, administered the Philadelphia YM and YWHA Camps from the 1920 through the 1960s and held a variety of offices in the American Camping Association nationally and in the Eastern Pennsylvania Section.

Doug Magnuson is a doctoral candidate in educational psychology at the University of Minnesota and earned his master's degree there in recreation, parks, and leisure studies. He grew up at camp; his father, Larry Magnuson, directed Camp Lebanon in Minnesota for ten years. Doug's camp and youth development experiences range from executive director of Salvation Army Camp Echo Grove to service as a group home "teaching parent," and program development and training for the Boy Scouts of America through its Ethics in Action project. Currently, Doug is working on the Project on Vocation, Work, and Youth Development at the College of St. Catherine in St. Paul and is an instructor in youth studies in the School of Social Work at the University of Minnesota.

Connie Magnuson holds a doctorate in education and a master's degree in recreation, parks, and leisure studies from the University of Minnesota. She has been on the faculties of a number of university recreation departments and has written and presented extensively on camp staff, including publication in *Camping Magazine.* Connie also grew up in a camp family; her parents, Elwyn and Donna Felt, were involved as camp volunteers throughout her childhood. Connie's camping-related experience includes being a community center director for the Salvation Army, day camp director for Central Place Community Center, food service director at Camp Echo Grove and Silver Lake Camp, group home "teaching parent," and trip leader and currently program director for Search Beyond Adventures, Inc., in Minneapolis. Connie is a former staff member of Christian Camping International and board member of the American Camping Association Northland Section.

David Beker holds a master of social work degree from Yeshiva University and has held a variety of youth work and social work positions, including several years as a camp counselor and as program director at a youth leadership development camp associated with Camp Moshava in Pennsylvania. After moving to Jerusalem in 1994, David served as administrator at a residential religious school and as a direct care worker and social worker in a group home for the developmentally disabled. He is currently an Israel Advisor for Yeshiva University students studying there.

Jerry Beker, David E. Beker, Connie Magnuson, and Doug Magnuson